C0-AZS-032

Toronto 6 Sketches

FOR MY MOTHER

MIKE FILEY

Toronto Sketches 6

"The Way We Were"
Columns from the *Toronto Sunday Sun*

DUNDURN PRESS
TORONTO · OXFORD

Copyright © Mike Filey, 2000

All rights reserved. No part of this publication may be reproduced, stored in a retrieval system, or transmitted in any form or by any means, electronic, mechanical, photocopying, recording, or otherwise (except for brief passages for purposes of review) without the prior permission of Dundurn Press. Permission to photocopy should be requested from the Canadian Copyright Licensing Agency.

Editor: Edna Barker
Design: Jessica Hexham
Printer: Webcom

Canadian Cataloguing in Publication Data

Filey, Mike, 1941-
    Toronto sketches 6: "the way we were"

ISBN 1-55002-339-X

1. Toronto (Ont.) — History. I. Title.

FC3097.4.F5493 2000   971.3'541   C00-931870-4   F1059.57F554 2000

1   2   3   4   5   04   03   02   01   00

ONTARIO ARTS COUNCIL
CONSEIL DES ARTS DE L'ONTARIO

We acknowledge the support of the **Canada Council for the Arts** and the **Ontario Arts Council** for our publishing program. We also acknowledge the financial support of the **Government of Canada** through the **Book Publishing Industry Development Program, The Association for the Export of Canadian Books**, and the **Government of Ontario** through the **Ontario Book Publishers Tax Credit** program.

Care has been taken to trace the ownership of copyright material used in this book. The author and the publisher welcome any information enabling them to rectify any references or credit in subsequent editions.
                                                                    J. Kirk Howard, President

Printed and bound in Canada.⊗
Printed on recycled paper.

www.dundurn.com

Dundurn Press
8 Market Street
Suite 200
Toronto, Ontario, Canada
M5E 1M6

Dundurn Press
73 Lime Walk
Headington, Oxford,
England
OX3 7AD

Dundurn Press
2250 Military Road
Tonawanda NY
U.S.A. 14150

Contents

FOREWORD by Paul Godfrey   8

ACKNOWLEDGEMENTS   9

IS THIS THE SAME CAR? January 5, 1997   11

TORONTO'S FAMOUS CASA LOMA January 12, 1997   14

HOSPITAL DREAM DIES January 19, 1997   17

IT ALL SOUNDS FAMILIAR January 26, 1997   20

LIGHTS, CAMERA... February 2, 1997   23

POSTAL DESIGN ON AVIATION HISTORY February 9, 1997   26

IT'S WHEEL FASCINATIN' February 16, 1997   29

BUILDING A LASTING NAME February 23, 1997   32

MILK RUN MEMORIES March 2, 1997   35

A RETAIL SURVIVOR March 9, 1997   38

GONE UP IN SMOKE March 16, 1997   42

MORE CANADIAN AVIATION HISTORY March 27, 1997   45

NATIONAL TRADE CENTRE SET TO OPEN March 30, 1997   47

A PIECE OF HISTORY IS ON THE MOVE April 6, 1997   50

PLAYIN' BALL WITH CUBA April 13, 1997   54

SUNNYBROOK ESTABLISHED TO HEAL WAR'S
         WOUNDED April 20, 1997   58

A GALLANT SHIP REMEMBERED April 27, 1997   62

A GIFTED FUNNYMAN May 4, 1997   65

WILL IT ARRIVE ON TIME? May 11, 1997   68

HOW SUNDAY STREETCAR SERVICE GOT ON TRACK May 18, 1997   71

MOVING AHEAD WITH GO May 25, 1997   74

READY FOR TAKEOFF June 1, 1997   78

TIDY'S REMAINS A THRIVING ENTERPRISE June 8, 1997   81

A GIFTED ENTERTAINER June 15, 1997   83

NEW BELLS ARE READY TO PEAL AT ST. JAMES' June 21, 1997   86

SUNNYSIDE'S 75TH ANNIVERSARY June 28, 1997   89

DEDICATED TO ANARCHY June 29, 1997   91

YES, SIR HENRY'S HOME REALLY WAS HIS CASTLE July 6, 1997   94

REMEMBERING SUNNY DAYS GONE BY July 20, 1997   97

TRACK TO THE FUTURE July 27, 1997   99

MACKENZIE'S MANSIONS August 3, 1997   101

TAKING A MILK RUN ALONG SPADINA August 10, 1997   104

I REMEMBER A VERY SPECIAL EX August 17, 1997   107

CNE'S HERITAGE IS ON DISPLAY August 24, 1997   110

REMEMBERING THE OTHER PRINCE August 31, 1997   114

HERE'S WHERE YOU SERVED YOUR TIME September 7, 1997   118

WHALE SIGHTING IN TORONTO   September 14, 1997   122
SHE WAS A MUSICAL SWEETHEART   September 28, 1997   125
THE LAUGH'S ON US   October 5, 1997   128
ROADS TOOK THEIR TOLL IN EARLY T.O.   October 12, 1997   132
CRUISE SHIP REVIVAL ON GREAT LAKES   October 19, 1997   135
RAISE A GLASS TO THE SILVER RAIL   October 26, 1997   138
GROWING UP WITH CANADIAN TIRE   November 2, 1997   141
IT'S A RIGHT ROYAL ANNIVERSARY   November 9, 1997   145
PEOPLE POWER SAVES STREETCARS   November 16, 1997   148
MUSIC MAN OF THE CANADIAN ARMY   November 23, 1997   152
PART OF OUR PAST DISTILLED THROUGH
        FLATIRON BUILDING   November 30, 1997   155
MEMORIES OF CHRISTMAS PAST   December 21, 1997   158
EVOLUTION OF A "MEETING PLACE"   December 28, 1997   161
THE MORE THINGS CHANGE...   January 4, 1998   164
THE TRAGIC TRUTH   January 11, 1998   166
MORE TALES OF THE TITANIC   January 18, 1998   169
A SPIN DOWN AUTO ROW   January 25, 1998   172
MEASURE OF SUCCESS   February 8, 1998   175
TORONTO AUTO SHOWS HAVE
        ALWAYS BEEN POPULAR   February 15, 1998   178
BAYVIEW GHOSTS STILL HAUNT TORONTO   February 22, 1998   181
LIVING HIGH OFF HOGTOWN'S PAST   March 1, 1998   184
MEET THE KNIGHT WHO BUILT OUR CASTLE   March 8, 1998   187
SPORTSMEN'S SHOW TURNS 50   March 15, 1998   190
THEY'RE STILL COOKIN' WITH GAS   March 22, 1998   193
BIG SHOTS BACK IN SHIPSHAPE   March 29, 1998   196
T.O. PAPER CARRIED TITANIC SCOOP   April 12, 1998   200
MICHIE'S TRADITION OF WEALTH AND PRESTIGE   April 19, 1998   203
TEMPORARY WAR TAX NOW ECONOMIC
        CORNERSTONE   April 26, 1998   206
MEET OUR FIRST TAXMAN   May 3, 1998   209
THEY'RE TORONTO'S OWN GUIDING LIGHTS   May 10, 1998   212
WHAT'S IN A NAME? PLENTY   May 17, 1998   215
THE SINKING OF A CANADIAN DREAM   May 24, 1998   218
TORONTO'S STORMY PAST   May 31, 1998   222
AN IMPORTANT CORNER IN TORONTO'S HISTORY
        June 7, 1998   225
A STREETCAR NAMED PETER WITT   July 5, 1998   228
BRIDGING THE GAP TO THE DANFORTH   July 12, 1998   231
ROY ROGERS' HAPPY TRAILS LED TO TORONTO   July 19, 1998   234

BRIDGE TO CANADA'S SUPERHIGHWAYS July 26, 1998   237
ON THE RIGHT TRACK August 2, 1998   240
TRAFFIC STOPPERS August 9, 1998   243
ALL ABOARD FOR A TRIP INTO THE PAST August 16, 1998   246
AIRPORT MEMORIES TAKE FLIGHT August 23, 1998   250
IT'S THE WHEEL THING AT THE CNE August 30, 1998   253
FAREWELL TO A CNE LANDMARK September 6, 1998   256
MAJOR MACKENZIE'S HOME NOW PART OF
      PIONEER PAST September 13, 1998   259
A PALATIAL SCHEME WITHOUT PIER September 20, 1998   262
THE HOUSES THAT BISHOP BUILT September 27, 1998   265
STREET STANDS FRONT AND CENTRE October 4, 1998   268
1915 FORD FIT TO A "T" October 11, 1998   271
MYSTERY PHOTO IS AN HISTORICAL GEM October 18, 1998   274
CITY'S PAST VANISHES WITH ARRIVAL OF
      NEW BUILDINGS October 25, 1998   276
FILLING USED TO BE A JOY AT THE PUMPS November 1, 1998   279
SANTA CLAUS ALWAYS WELCOME IN TORONTO November 15, 1998   281
TIMELY COTTAGE DOWN BY THE BAY December 13, 1998   284
WHEN THE SNOW REALLY WAS WAISTDEEP December 20, 1998   287
OUT WITH THE NEW, IN WITH THE OLD December 27, 1998   291

Foreword

I am most honoured to comment on Mike Filey's latest book on this, his 25th year of writing for the Sunday Sun.

Mike's column first appeared on a regular basis back in 1975, and over the years he has become the top and most respected Toronto historian.

I was always fascinated by Mike Filey's interest in The Way We Were (our history) and often quoted many of his columns during my years as the Chairman of Metro Toronto.

Filey's keen historical perspective is significant in shedding light on how certain events unfolded in Toronto.

In the last twenty-five years, Toronto has grown from a city that was viewed as secondary to Montreal, but has now sprung forward to become one of the great leading cities of the world. In the last two and a half decades, we have certainly built a community that is relatively safe, has excellent transportation, few, if any, slums, and most of all, a quality of life that is second to none. People of multipleraces, creeds, and colour make up our community. We are not a melting pot, but rather a mosaic — all living together in harmony and working towards building a stronger and more progressive city.

Filey, whose work has focussed on how we have changed over the last one hundred years, often brings to our attention many interesting tidbits of information. I have often used his historical information in my speeches or in trivia contests. I never knew Bay Street was once known as Bear Street. It was a question that was asked of my son during one of his assignments at Crescent School. We were stumped but Filey knew the answer instantly.

Besides being a most livable community made up of all the important essential services, Toronto is socially complete, culturally complete, and athletically complete — a city that is most unique among its counterparts.

I have had the wonderful honour of being Chairman of Metro Toronto for eleven years, from 1973 to 1984. The city has been blessed in having someone who really cares about our past, our present, and our future in Mike Filey. He is one of our great citizens and, of course, a great historian.

Paul Godfrey, CM
President and CEO, SUN MEDIA Corporation, 1984–2000

Acknowledgements

As always, people at the *Sun* have made my work that much easier and that much more fun. In particular, I'd like to thank Marilyn Linton and Vena Eaton of the Lifestyle section and Ed Piwowarczyk of the Features Desk, each of whom ensures that my material actually makes it into the Sunday paper and looks good when it gets there. Researching material for each week's column results in extended periods in the *Sun*'s library (tax man, please note). It could be a drag, but thanks to head librarian Julie Kirsh and her little helpers — Katherine, Glenna, Gillian, Joyce, and Sue — for both their help and tolerance. A special thanks to Jeff Rickard, one of the *Sun*'s computer specialists whose expertise keeps my bits and bytes from running all over my RAM and ROM. By the way, Jeff now has his own business if you too need help.

Thanks also to the good people at Dundurn Press, who strive to turn out that vanishing breed of books — you know, the ones about our great country. It's a tough and often thankless job, but someone has to do it. Dundurn does it well.

And finally, I'm always on the lookout for story ideas as well as interesting old photographs of our city. If you have some of either and would like to share them with my *Sun* readers, drop me a note c/o the paper or the publisher.

Once again, thanks to my wife, proofreader, typist, and best fan, Yarmila.

Mike Filey

Angelo Spadafore's Toronto-built Russell automobile in front of Eglinton Methodist Church on Yonge Street in North Toronto, c. 1914.

Russell automobile stuck in the Yonge Street mud sometime in 1913. Same car?

IS THIS THE SAME CAR?

January 5, 1997

Soon after I ran a photo taken in 1913 of a West Toronto built Russell automobile stuck in the mud on Yonge Street somewhere in North Toronto (a town that one year earlier had been annexed by the big City of Toronto), reader George Spadafore sent a photo from his collection showing a similar automobile parked in front of Eglinton Methodist Church. This old church was located on the east side of Yonge Street at the Glengrove Avenue corner. (In 1926 the congregation moved into their new church on Sheldrake Boulevard.) In George's undated photo his father Angelo poses proudly behind the wheel. Angelo Spadafore was born in Italy in 1896, emigrated to Washington State then to Toronto, where he obtained employment as a driver for a munitions company. Is it possible that the same car (with different owners) appears in both photos? Any old car buffs out there think that's possible?

I received several answers to my question. While the cars are similar, several buffs pointed out minor differences (number of wheel spokes and the shape of the headlights) that confirm the two cars are different.

****

For those of us who delve into the history of our great city, the ongoing rhetoric about whether the amalgamation of the existing half dozen communities that make up the present Metropolitan Toronto federation into one unified city is a good or bad move immediately prompts the question, "Where have I heard this all before"? A quick perusal of the files and old newspapers reveals that the matter is not a new subject.

What follows are a few brief story excerpts or headlines taken from city papers of the past. All point to the imminent creation of "one" Toronto.

- *Annexation of York and East York is likely to receive the consideration of this year's Toronto city council.* January 4, 1930.
- *To attempt a defence of existing multiple units of government is ridiculous.* York County Council Minutes, 1934

City and provincial leaders agreed yesterday that Toronto and its surrounding suburban municipalities should get together on an amalgamation scheme. September 22, 1949

- *Spectacular expansion of Toronto city boundary lines to take in 7 [adjacent] municipalities is recommended in a plan submitted by the Toronto and York Planning Board today.* December 5, 1949

- *Application to the Ontario Municipal board for progressive amalgamation with Toronto of the neighbouring municipalities was recommended to City Council today by the Board of Control.* January 30, 1950

- *Toronto applies to the provincial government for total amalgamation with surrounding municipalities.* May 15, 1950

- *Unless they amalgamate with Toronto North York, Etobicoke and Scarborough may be diminished by the successive secession of their more populous areas.* October 13, 1950

- *The ultimate in [Metropolitan Toronto] unity would be amalgamation of the municipalities that make up the Metro area into one big city.* January 18, 1960.

- *One of the great issues in the upcoming civic election is amalgamation. Should Toronto and the suburban municipalities be united to for one big city or should the Metro system be retained and the area go on developing as it is now - balkanized, over-governed, wastefully governed, inefficiently governed.* November 30, 1960

- *Amalgamation of the area municipalities could be carried out and services improved at a net tax reduction of 3 mils for Toronto homeowners.* April 8, 1964

So whether you believe that unification will be good or bad for our community one thing is obvious. It's certainly not a new idea. What is new, however, is that we now have a government that's prepared to act on a matter that's been discussed for more than half a century. By the way, for what it's worth, I believe the unification process is long overdue.

It's interesting to look at the evolution of the present City of Toronto since its birth on March 6, 1834. For almost half a century, the city boundaries remained constant, but as more and more people moved into the surrounding suburban communities, these same communities, crying financial hardship, began to plead with Toronto officials to annex them and provide the physical necessities of life — sidewalks, sewers, a supply of potable water, and so on.

The first in was the Town of Yorkville (February 1, 1883), followed by the communities of Brockton, Riverdale, Rosedale, Sunnyside,

Parkdale, Deer Park, Balmy Beach, Earlscourt, and Dovercourt. These annexations ended when the Town of North Toronto became part of Toronto on December 15, 1912. Interestingly, and contrary to those who claim Metro's neighbourhoods will lose their identity when a unified Toronto comes into being next year, every one of the communities I've just mentioned is still very much alive.

The "new" City of Toronto, incorporating the former cities of Toronto, Scarborough, Etobicoke, North York, York, and the Borough of East York, came into being on January 1, 1998.

TORONTO'S FAMOUS CASA LOMA

January 12, 1997

O ne of my favourite television programs is "America's Castles," a show that appears on the Arts & Entertainment Network every Sunday night at ten o'clock. Each week a magnificent baronial residence located somewhere in the United States is featured.

Casa Loma, seen here under construction in 1913, was built to host royalty. Today, it's one of Toronto's top tourist attractions.

George Washington Vanderbilt II's 1890–1895 creation Biltmore House in North Carolina and Randolph Hearst's $50 million La Cuesta Encantata near San Simeon, California, are but two of the many "castles" that have been featured. The vast majority have been located in the United States.

Tonight it's our turn as the show travels north of the border to spotlight Toronto's very own castle, Casa Loma. I participated in the taping last summer, but not having previewed the show don't know what was kept in or cut out. We'll see.

Actually, the very idea that Casa Loma would make a perfect subject for the program is not the least bit surprising to me. One afternoon while conducting a group of American visitors around Toronto, as I frequently do, the question as to just how much our friends south of the border knew about Toronto came up.

One woman, a resident of Kansas, the Sunflower State, volunteered that prior to her arrival she knew just two things about our city. She knew we had a baseball team (the Blue Jays just having won the World Series again) and that Toronto was the home of a place called Casa Loma. And now she was actually going to visit it! Imagine. Just the Blue Jays and Casa Loma.

Even though it's hard to picture our city without this unique landmark, there was a time when the future of Sir Henry's Pellatt's palatial home on the hill was in considerable doubt. In fact, if some city officials had had their way many years ago, there'd be no reason for "America's Castles" to visit Toronto at all, since there'd be no Casa Loma. But let me start at the beginning.

Henry Pellatt was born in Kingston, Ontario, in 1859. At the age of just two he journeyed to Toronto with his parents, where the elder Pellatt entered the stocks and bonds business. After receiving a formal education at the city's Model School young Henry joined the firm in 1876, becoming a full partner in 1883.

It didn't take long for the young man to make a name for himself in the financial world. His original fortune of between $300 000 and $400 000 followed astute real estate investments in western Canada where 1.5 million acres of land deeded by the government to the fledgling CPR were offered for sale. Pellatt bought thousands at individual share prices of between $10 and $12, eventually selling most for as much as $90 a share.

Great sums of money came to Henry from other sources — electricity, mining, and the stock market to name just a few. But he would lose great sums, as well. That setback, however, was still some years in the future.

One of Henry's favourite pastimes was playing soldier, and as the nation's foremost royalist he spent thousands on his beloved Queen's Own Rifles. In 1902 he took the entire military band to the coronation of King George V, and eight years later accompanied 670 members of the regiment to England to participate in the British Army's autumn manoeuvres. Both times he did it out of his own pocket!

But Sir Henry's (he was elevated to the peerage in 1905) everlasting claim to fame will be his residence on a fifteen-acre piece of property (even then referred to as Casa Loma) on a rise of land north of the city known in recent history as Well's Hill, but historically as Spadina, a word derived from the native Indian *Ishapadenah*, "little hill." It was here that his beloved monarch could live in splendour during future visits to Toronto.

First, though, would come the stables and coach house, followed in 1910 by work on the new residence's foundations. Torontonians had never seen anything like it, and for the next three years they would venture into the countryside to watch what some called "Pellatt's folly" take shape. Sir Henry and his wife finally took up residence in 1913, only to move out a decade later when stock market and other financial setbacks plus exorbitant living costs at the castle (heating bills of $15 000 a year and something called "market value reassessment" that had resulted in the annual property tax bill rising from $600 in 1914 to $12 000 in the twenties) forced him to abandon Casa Loma.

The city became the reluctant owner, and while several intriguing ideas as to what to do with the place were presented, a few city officials suggested it be demolished and the land on which it stood sold off.

Eventually architect turned entrepreneur William Sparling succeeded in running the place as an apartment hotel, only to be stymied by an unforeseen world depression.

In 1937, and almost out of desperation, the city allowed the Kiwanis Club of West Toronto to operate the castle as a tourist attraction. This was to be a stopgap measure until something else came up. Sixty years have passed, and the Kiwanis Club continues to operate Casa Loma with net proceeds earmarked for charitable uses. By the way, no reigning monarch has bothered to drop by for a visit.

HOSPITAL DREAM DIES

January 19, 1997

With all the talk about the downsizing or closure of some of our local hospitals, I was absolutely fascinated by a brief story that jumped off the microfilm reader screen as I perused an old Toronto *Telegram* newspaper in the *Sun* library the other day. Seems that back on September 22, 1964, a Toronto doctor by the name of John Fenn who, with several associates, had developed plans for a new city hospital, were still awaiting the government's final go-ahead. Their plan was to erect a $13-million, 21-storey, 567-bed hospital on a parcel of land they had assembled on the east side of Yonge Street between Balliol Street and Davisville Avenue (opposite the TTC's Davisville subway yards).

Architectural rendering of Toronto's proposed Fenway General Hospital on Yonge Street south of Davisville Avenue.

Knowing full well that the proposed structure was never built, I was curious as to what happened to derail it. I contacted the good doctor who, while obviously surprised by my phone call (after all, the plan had surfaced more than 30 years ago), graciously told me the rest of the story. Seems that even as the consortium was awaiting final approvals, plans were being formulated to transfer the lands and non-veterans' facilities of Sunnybrook Hospital on Bayview Avenue in North York to the University of Toronto for use as a community care, research, and teaching facility.

Sunnybrook, which had opened on June 12, 1948, had been built as a veterans' hospital to replace the ancient and totally unsuitable Christie Street Orthopedic Hospital downtown. However, as the years went by the occupancy rate dropped so that by the early 1960s only 45 percent of the beds were occupied. It was obvious that additional uses had to be found. What resulted was one of those good news, bad news stories, for while the community gained a new health-care facility, Dr. Fenn's dream of his own hospital, which the backers had planned to call Fenway General, ended.

****

The other afternoon while driving along Lawrence Avenue East near the Don Mills shopping centre I spied a sign that at first glance suggested a solution to the financial plight of our beleaguered transit system had finally been realized. There in large black and white letters were the words Subway Now Under New Management. Had we, in fact, returned to the days of yore when transit services were provided by a private company whose priority was to get the passenger's fare in the box without spending a lot of time, money, and effort getting him or her to their respective destinations? In fact wasn't it this public-be-damned attitude that would eventually see that monopoly terminated and a publicly owned TTC created? Surely, the politicians weren't"t falling into that trap again. As I stared at the sign, waiting for the traffic light to change, the penny dropped. It wasn't our subway system that was under new management. It was the Subway sandwich shop in the plaza. Whew!

****

Reader Andy Cobean wonders whether any other readers remember a restaurant on old Highway 27 near Dundas Street called Bert's

Turkey Palace. My aunt and uncle lived nearby and I vaguely recall the place. I do know that Hedges Boulevard in Etobicoke was named in Bert's honour. Anyone got other stories about the Turkey Palace, a photo perhaps?

A sign of the times?

IT ALL SOUNDS FAMILIAR

January 26, 1997

If nothing else, all this conjecture about whether the streamlining of our community into one so-called "megacity" (boy, I hate that term) will be, in the long term, good or bad for Toronto certainly gives me lots of new story ideas for this column. So step into my time machine and follow me back to the year 1953, when something called Metropolitan Toronto was (in some minds) being forced down the throats of local politicians by Premier Leslie Frost and the Conservative members of the provincial legislature. In fact, on February 2 of that year, 19 out of the 20 members on Toronto city council voted to oppose the province's plan to create a federation consisting of the City of Toronto and its 12 surrounding suburban neighbours. Only the mayor, someone named Allan Lamport, thought it was a good idea. As a result of that lopsided vote against the creation of Metro, the city politicians decided to forward a letter of protest to those in charge up at Queen's Park, and the city's solicitors were ordered to begin proceedings to have the government's action declared illegal.

Oh, there was one other thing those politicians demanded. They wanted to hold a plebiscite on the matter. It's interesting to note that while the city refused to consider the idea of a federation of neighbouring communities, it was all for amalgamating them into one giant "megacity." The resultant benefits, as spelled out in a series of newspaper ads, would be the creation one elected government instead of the 13 as then existed, the centralization and uniformity of services throughout the new city, and all municipal planning and zoning done by one authority. (Are you aware that today you can smoke in the Diana Sweets restaurant in Scarborough but not in the one in North York?) The most important advantage, as most taxpayers would agree (even those of today), was that the one-city concept would mean reduced administrative costs. Let me remind you, all this took place prior to the creation of Metro, 44 years ago!

Well, as we all know the province got its way and the new Municipality of Metropolitan Toronto came into being on January 1, 1954.

One of the first things the new Metro politicians under Fred Gardiner looked into was how best to improve the flow of traffic into, out of, and around the new metropolitan area. Harvey Rose, Metro's first Roads Commissioner, recommended that a total of 18 road improvement projects be started immediately. The budget he suggested that would allow this work to be undertaken amounted to $15 267 000, a figure that doesn't seem like much today, but for 1954 was an incredibly large amount. Priorities were set with the Lakeshore Expressway (now the Gardiner), the Spadina Parkway (from MacPherson Avenue to Wilson Avenue), the extension of Eglinton Avenue (west into Etobicoke and east into Scarborough), the Don Valley Parkway, and the widening of Avenue Road from Bloor Street to St. Clair Avenue making the top of the list.

Artist's concept of planner Norman Wilson's proposed Scarborough Bluffs Expressway, 1954.

This latter project, the widening of Avenue Road, has the distinction of being the first road improvement undertaken by the new Metro corporation. Work began on this $3-million project as soon as the streetcars on the Bay route (from the docks loop on Queen's Quay via Bay, Bloor, Avenue Road, St. Clair, to Earlscourt loop at Lansdowne) were removed coincident with the opening of the new Yonge subway on March 30, 1954.

While officials sorted out construction priorities, a new project was suddenly added to the mix. According to its proponent, Toronto born transportation consultant Norman Wilson, an "express highway" along the shore of Lake Ontario at the base of the Scarborough Bluffs would alleviate the nightmarish traffic problems that existed (and still exist) along Queen Street, Woodbine Avenue and Kingston Road in the southeast corner of Metro by connecting the Highland Creek area with the new Lakeshore Expressway. Actually, Wilson had first suggested building the highway back in 1923. Obviously there were no takers, but as traffic tie-ups in that part of town continued to deteriorate, his idea began to look more and more logical. Even Fred Gardiner, the persuasive Metro chairman, was convinced, as was Spencer Clarke, who believed the highway and a series of groins erected perpendicular to the roadway and jutting into the lake would help stop the progressive erosion of the Bluffs. Clarke was especially concerned with the erosion problem as he was the owner of the Guild of All Arts property (now the Guild Inn). Nevertheless, the $40-million construction figure was just too much for the young Metro. For a second, and quite likely the last time, the idea was shelved.

LIGHTS, CAMERA...

February 2, 1997

Ad for *The Man From Toronto*, an English-produced film that ran at the city's Tivoli theatre from August 19 to 25, 1933.

Have you ever been caught in one of those all too frequent traffic jams that turn out to be the result not of some unfortunate accident or fire, but occur because some film crew had decided that five in the afternoon was the perfect time to stall rush hour traffic so the crew could shoot an all-important scene for a movie of some made-for-TV production? (You can tell I'm still steaming over the fact that the producers of *Mrs. Winterbourne*, which was shot in various locations in and around Toronto and managed to tie things up good several times, never even had the good grace to mention our city in the movie credits, although both Boston and New York were listed.)

It's a sure bet that similar traffic problems didn't unfold when the producers were in town some years ago filming a little item titled *Satan's Paradise*. Actually, when that movie was being shot in Toronto cars and trucks would have been the least of the crew's problems. Horses may have been, though, since the year in question was 1923 with *Satan's Paradise* having the distinction of being the first feature-length movie to be filmed here in what has become Hollywood North.

Described by the press of the day as a seven-reel photodrama, *Satan's Paradise* by Sidney Hamilton was the latest, and the longest, in the Camera Classics series presented by Toronto's own Filmcraft studios. The movie, in which "fraudulent spiritualistic mediums are exposed for what they really are," featured an all Toronto cast with Clarence Quarrington as Ronald Gordon, Alice Dunn as Elsie Welford, his sweetheart, and a lady identified simply as Mrs. Houston as Ronald's mother. A news story reveals that this latter part was given to the first applicant answering an ad placed in the local newspapers by the film's producers because, as the paper divulged, "this wholesome Scotchwoman proved to be an ideal mother-type."

In short, the movie tells the story of a mother who, during the sad days of the Great War and even in spite of warnings from the family minister, is duped into believing Ronald, her supposedly dead soldier son, can be contacted by a spiritualist who then demands money from the mother in return for a string of messages from the beyond. Phew! Eventually, this fake is revealed by none other than Sidney Hamilton who, in addition to being the film's hero and star, is the same guy who produced the film and wrote the story. And yes, son Ronald makes it home, back from the front so to speak, at the end of the film. And they all live happily ever after, except the fake fakir, that is.

Locations selected for some of the outdoor scenes included views of Jarvis Street as well as streets in North Toronto and Weston. In fact, it was the residence of Dr. William Charlton, the well-known Weston doctor (and at one time town mayor), that was used for many of the film's interior shots. That house still stands at 89 Rosemount Avenue. Perhaps it should be plaqued or something.

While I have yet to confirm whether this film was ever screened anywhere, it was exactly 10 years later that Toronto definitely made it to the screen of the long demolished Tivoli theatre at Richmond

Dr. William Charlton's residence at 89 Rosemount Avenue in Weston was prominently featured in the first feature film to be shot in Toronto.

and Victoria streets. It was on August 19, 1933, that the new English comedy *The Man From Toronto* opened, the movie having been adapted from Douglas Murray's successful stage play of the same name. The movies stars were Jessie Matthews and Ian Hunter, both of whom would appear in a succession of popular English films. Their faces are probably familiar to those who watch the late late shows on TV.

Incidentally, that man from Toronto (as played by Ian Hunter) can inherit his uncle's fortune only if he journeys from Toronto to England and is able to both woo and marry an English lass (Jessie Matthews) who had been selected as the Torontonian's future wife by the rich uncle. What?

Ian Hunter and Jessie Matthews, the male and female stars of the film.

POSTAL DESIGN ON AVIATION HISTORY

Febraury 9, 1997

With all the hype surrounding the recent CBC mini-series on Canada's spectacular Avro Arrow, I'm sure most people feel they've read, heard, or seen just about everything connected with the rise and fall of that mighty aircraft. So did I until I came across the following piece of rather obscure Arrow trivia. The plane continued to take a licking well after it was cancelled by the Diefenbaker boys up in Ottawa.

Reproduction of the five-cent stamp commemorating the fiftieth anniversary of powered flight in Canada. The RCAF said the delta wing fighter was the Arrow. The post office said that the resemblance was just a coincidence.

In 1959, when postal officials decided to release a special five-cent stamp (remember when stamps were just a nickel?) to commemorate the fiftieth anniversary of powered flight in Canada, the choice of one of the aircraft that would appear on the new stamp was obvious. It had to be Canada's little Silver Dart, the creation of the Aerial Experimental Association that had been established by Alexander Graham Bell (yup, that one) in 1907. It was on February 23, 1909, that the little biplane, with Nova Scotia born, Toronto educated J.A.D. McCurdy clutching its primitive control stick, skimmed across the frozen bay at Baddeck,

Nova Scotia. Then, in full view of dozens of curious onlookers, the Silver Dart slowly but surely lifted off its runners and took to the air. At first the crowd stood spellbound, then realizing what they had witnessed broke into polite applause. Bell and his Aerial Experimental Association colleagues simply grinned and shook hands. As far as they were concerned the months of experimentation had assured them that the trial flight would be a success.

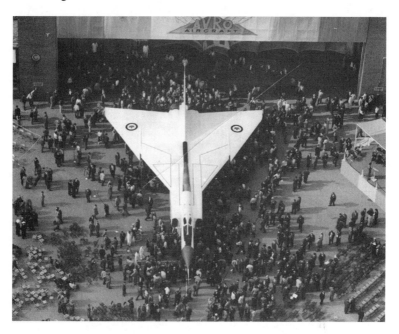

The real Arrow meets its public, October 4, 1957.

That half-mile flight of the Silver Dart on a cold February day in 1909 would enter the history books not only as the first public demonstration of powered flight in Canada, but it would also be recorded as the first powered flight in the entire British Commonwealth. The choice of the Silver Dart to grace the new stamp was obvious.

On the very day Canada's new commemorative stamp was announced, December 27, 1958, all systems were go at the sprawling Avro plant adjacent to the runways at Malton Airport northwest of Toronto. All five of the company's revolutionary new CF-105 Arrows had flown numerous times since 25201's maiden flight on March 25, 1958. In fact, Arrow 25202 had attained Mach 1.96 (or almost twice the speed of sound) just a month or so earlier. With all the successes thus far there was absolutely no doubt that, with the new Orenda Iroquois engine almost ready for installation and testing in the nearly complete Arrow number six (25206), all sorts of world records would soon be set in the cold, clear skies over Canada.

With Canada's Arrow program meeting or exceeding all objectives, postal officials had little difficulty in selecting the other aircraft that would share their new stamp that was scheduled for release on February 23, 1959. It had to be the Arrow. And that choice was just great with Avro officials for while the Arrow was doing everything they had hoped, the government had yet to give the green light to full-scale production. The stamp would certainly be a forceful addition to the company's campaign to get the government to make up its mind.

Meanwhile friction was mounting between RCAF and post office officials with the former claiming the latter had jumped the gun when it decided to feature an aircraft that had yet to be accepted on strength by the air force. The post office countered that they had simply chosen a delta wing aircraft. Any similarity to the Arrow was purely coincidental.

That bickering didn't really matter, after all, since the Arrow died (or was killed) on February 20, 1959, a mere three days before the stamp went on public sale. And in a rather strange twist of fate the plane's demise occurred exactly fifty years and three days after the historic flight of the Silver Dart.

IT'S WHEEL FASCINATIN'

February 16, 1997

Before car shows moved indoors, Toronto city streets were venues for impromptu displays. Here, a 1904 Winton in front of the dealer's showroom on Temperance Street draws a crowd of pioneer car buffs.

Once again thousands of Torontonians and visitors to our city are expected to visit the Canadian International Auto Show, which opened at the Metro Convention Centre on Front Street West. More than 1 000 vehicles of all types, sizes, and shapes will be on display, a spectacular increase over the 300 or so that were present when the show was first presented back in 1974 at what was then called the Toronto International Centre of Commerce across from Toronto International Airport.

But the public's fascination with cars and trucks in this town certainly didn't start as recently as 1974, as those who remember when the main reason for attending each year's CNE was to drool over the myriad vehicles on public display for the first time in the imposing Automotive Building. That structure, which has now been incorporated into the sprawling National Trade Centre at Exhibition Place, was added to the fair's ever-growing line-up of exhibit halls in

1929 and was to become home to the annual car show for almost four decades. However, when the dates of the annual fair were advanced to take advantage of better weather and the many tourists in town, the cars on display became, in effect, last year's models. That ultimately led to the demise of the annual CNE car show in 1967. Seven years later the Canadian International Auto Show debuted.

The unmistakable 1958 Edsel on public display for the first time at the 1957 CNE.

And here's an interesting piece of Canadian car show trivia. It was in the CNE's Automotive Building that the brand new Ford Edsel (the name was selected from a list of 6 000 possibilities) was seen by the public for the first time. Proving the importance of the Ex as the showplace of the nation, that world-premier event occurred on Monday, September 2, 1958, a full two days before "Edsel Day" south of the border. On that day the new 1958 Edsel Ranger, Pacer, Corsair and Citation models (priced from $2 519 to $3 801 US) joining a gaggle of year-old Ford Fairlanes, Meteor Rideaus, Mercury Turnpike Cruisers, Monarch Montcalms, Prefects, Consuls, and so on, in the Ford display area. The Edsels were on public display until the following Saturday when they were removed and put under wraps. They reappeared the following Wednesday in dealer showrooms ready for the expected hordes of customers who, unfortunately, didn't appear in the numbers anticipated. In fact, so few showed up in showrooms here and in the States that on November 19, 1959 the Edsel program was cancelled. Today, while only a small percentage of the 84 000 Edsels produced are still around those that are sell for a small fortune.

Before the Automotive Building opened in 1929, the CNE had featured an automobile show in the ancient (1908) Transportation

Building located south of the Dufferin Gate. As the number of items grew to include bicycles, motorcycles, and even aeroplanes (to use the spelling of the period) and motorboats, the building ran out of space and several large tents were erected nearby. The Transportation Building (also known as the International Building, then the Business Machines Building, and finally the Spanish Pavilion) was destroyed by fire in 1974, coincidentally the same year that the Canadian International Auto Show was born near the airport. It was also a year I'll remember, as that was the year I joined the staff of the CNE, and the TTC went out on strike coincident with my arrival and the fair's opening. Some wags suggested that my arrival at the Ex, the fire, and the strike were somehow connected. Not so!

Autos shows weren't just the purview of the annual CNE. In fact, the city's pioneer auto show in 1906 attracted hundreds of viewers to the old Granite Club rink on Church Street. Those crowds mushroomed into thousands of gawkers when the show was moved into the huge Armouries on University Avenue, a site now occupied by the Court House. A historic plaque and nearby street name recognize the castle-like structure that was a city landmark until its unfortunate demolition in 1963. So successful was the show at this new site that the 1911 edition was hailed as "the Dominion's largest and most elaborate [auto show] with the 350 vehicles on display, ranging in price as they do from $500 to $10,000 and having a total value of nearly a million dollars, [representing] the best in English, French, Belgian, German, American and Canadian workmanship."

BUILDING A LASTING NAME

February 23, 1997

The Commercial Bank of the Midland District as it looked before being disassembled,
stored, and reassembled inside the newly erected BCE Place.

Nestled inside one of downtown Toronto's newest and most modern skyscrapers is one of the community's oldest buildings, which, in its time, was a structure of importance. Encased as it is within the magnificent vaulted atrium of BCE Place, the presence of the 1844 Commercial Bank of the Midland District comes as a bit of shock to those visiting the office tower and shopping and dining complex for the first time. Conversely, frequent visitors seem to enjoy the juxtaposition of the ancient and the new. And I have no doubt that the building's architect, English born William Thomas, would be pleased to learn that not only does his creation still stand, but that it has once again gained a place of prominence as the Toronto office of the Canadian Chamber of Commerce.

Born in Suffolk, England, in 1799, Thomas served his apprenticeship in various building trades in Chalford, Gloucestershire.

Eventually he moved to the bustling City of Birmingham where he obtained work as a builder joiner. He was to find his true calling following a visit to Leamington Spa, where the discovery of the soothing and healing effects of water from the local saltwater wells was transforming the sleepy little village into a bustling community sadly lacking in proper accommodation for the wealthy who were moving into the fashionable spa town. Modern-day visitors to Leamington Spa can still inspect some of the young architect's earliest endeavours.

Architect William Thomas (1799-1860)

Unfortunately, severe financial setbacks forced Thomas to seek his future as an architect in the New World. Following a three-week ocean crossing, the Thomas family arrived in New York, struck out for the British colony of Canada West, and arrived in the capital city of Toronto, population 15 000, in 1843. Here he would vie for work with a trio of architects, one of whom, John George Howard, is better recognized as the original owner of Colborne Lodge, constructed within his sprawling country estate, which we know today as High Park.

Thomas's impact on the physical appearance of his adopted city was remarkable, with many of his works still very much in evidence — for example St. Michael's Cathedral on Shuter Street, St. Lawrence Hall at King and Jarvis streets, Oakham House at the southwest corner of Church and Gould streets (erected in 1848 as Thomas's residence in the northern reaches of the city), the House of Industry on Elm Street, St. George's Church on Dundas Street in Etobicoke, and the oldest part of the Don Jail (which was budgeted at $96 000, but, as a result of government interference and bungling, whose final cost was $267 000!) Other Thomas creations graced streets in Hamilton, Halifax, Paris, and Goderich. Visitors to the Niagara area can see his work in the Court House in Niagara-on-the-Lake and in Brock's Monument on the heights at Queenston. William Thomas died on December 28, 1860.

The historic bank building can now be found inside BCE Place.

MILK RUN MEMORIES

March 2, 1997

What do the following names have in common — Caulfield, Donlands, Blantyre, Briar Hill, City, Olive Farm, and Birney? For long-time Torontonians it's really no contest, as I'm sure most will quickly recognize one or more of these names as dairies that use to deliver milk and other dairy products using horse-drawn wagons (and eventually motorized vehicles) right to the house (or in many cases right to the milk box). For those of you who might have been thrown by that last name, Birney, don't worry. Messrs John and Joseph Birney have the distinction of being Toronto's very first dairymen, and the fact that the year they started in business was 1867 no doubt accounts for few, if any, readers recognizing the name.

Uplands Dairy use to bring milk and other dairy products right to the door. The company was located on Mt. Pleasant Road just south of Eglinton. And remember those phone number prefixes? MO was Mohawk.

This little trivia quiz is simply to introduce you to a book written by Dave Thomas and Bob Marchant and published by Cowtown Publications. *When Milk Came in Bottles* relates the fascinating history of the once highly diversified dairy business that flourished in and around Toronto until business efficiencies dictated that many either close or be taken over by a few of the larger operators. For instance Olive Farm ("You can whip our cream, but can't beat our milk"), Rogers, and Hall's vanished while City (whose large plant still stands on the east side of Spadina Crescent north of College), Caulfield's, and Cloverdale became part of Borden's, which was subsequently absorbed by Silverwood Dairy. Then, in 1983, the latter became part of Ault Foods. And next?

The Eaton Centre that wasn't. Note that the old City Hall is missing though its clock tower and Cenotaph are still there. Also visible are the new City Hall as well as the proposed circular convention hotel and office and apartment towers.

You know you're getting older when buildings you watched going up have always been there for many of your colleagues. That fact of life hit home hard the other day while I was chatting with a couple of co-op students from West Toronto Collegiate who are gaining work experience at the Toronto *Sun*. I was researching the story of the Eaton Centre in the newspaper's library where they overheard me say that it doesn't seem possible this landmark has been open for 20 years. For them it had always been there.

Interestingly, Toronto just about didn't get an Eaton Centre at all. And we certainly didn't get the one that John David Eaton and his developers originally had in mind back in the fall of 1965. That one was to cover almost all of the 15-acre Queen, Bay, Dundas, Yonge block and would have featured a 59-storey apartment and office tower, two 57-storey plus one 32-storey office buildings, a mammoth shopping mall with at least 200 stores, a 500-room convention hotel, a new bus terminal and (this is no surprise) a new Eaton's store that was described in the prospectus as the largest retail building in the world. This project, pegged at $250 million and identified by the more specific T. Eaton Centre title (emphasizing the initial T) would have required the demolition of old City Hall, although its Cenotaph and the historic Church of the Holy Trinity in the middle of the block were to be retained.

It was thought that this megaproject would also have resulted in the on-again, off-again Queen Street subway finally being built.

Well, what was first proclaimed as a project that would make Toronto "the city of the century" was soon the subject of all manner of criticism. By mid-May, 1967 the first attempt at an Eaton Centre was dead.

The planners and developers returned to City Hall a few years later with a scaled-down plan that was also subjected to immense scrutiny, but this time, the new concept was approved, thanks, in part, to the decision to retain the old City Hall in its entirety. Phase One of this version of the Eaton Centre (from Albert Way north to Dundas Street) opened on February 10, 1977. Phase Two (Queen Street to Albert Way) opened two years later.

A RETAIL SURVIVOR

March 9, 1997

The other Eaton store at 86 Yonge Street is visible in this ancient view of lower Yonge Street.

E arlier this month a shudder was felt throughout the country when Eaton's executives announced that the company was going to court to seek bankruptcy protection. Sure, other Canadian companies have suffered financial setbacks, a few fatal, but somehow the Eaton's problem hit closer to home. It was almost as if a member of the family had stumbled into serious financial difficulties. After all, Eaton's has been around almost as long as there's been a Canada, young Timothy having opened his first Toronto store less than 30 months after Ontario, Quebec, Nova Scotia, and New Brunswick joined together in Confederation. And

Timothy Eaton's year of birth being the same year the City of Toronto came into being gives the store another close connection with our city.

I think all Canadians hope and believe that this famous Canadian institution can and will weather this financial storm and will be around for at least another 127 years.

Timothy Eaton (1834-1907)

In her fascinating book on the life and times of Timothy Eaton (*Timothy Eaton and the Rise of His Department Store*, University of Toronto Press, 1990), author Joy Santink documents the story of the 35-year-old's arrival in Toronto in early 1869. After a short stint in the wholesale dry goods business at 8 Front Street West, Timothy rethought his future and on December 9 of that year opened a department store at 178 Yonge Street (a site later occupied by his competitor Robert Simpson and later still by The Bay). This one-stop shopping concept (to use present-day terminology), which he established in the city's new shopping district (King Street had for years been the traditional shopping area), quickly began to play havoc with the usual practice of visiting separate shops for specific items. On several occasions those who were feeling the impact of Eaton's new way of doing business attempted to have city officials come to their aid by assessing the Eaton store, the stock, and anything else that might increase his taxes and ultimately force the newcomer to move on. Eaton also faced possible financial ruin when initial sales figures failed to meet expectations. Earlier experiences with rural shoppers in his Kirkton and St. Mary's, Ontario, stores were quite different from the needs of the more sophisticated Toronto shoppers. Soon his bills began to exceed store income by a significant margin, but there was no doubt that Timothy was in it for the long run. He persevered and eventually sales figures began to take off. And as business grew so too did the need for additional space and in 1883 a site in the old Page Block on the west side of Yonge north of Queen was acquired. Over the next four years the store continually underwent expansion until virtually all of the Yonge, Queen, James, and Albert block was occupied by the growing Eaton store. It wasn't until early 1977, when the new Eaton store opened at the north end of the Eaton Centre, that the Yonge and Queen site was vacated.

Examination of the Eaton family's early days in Toronto reveals that there was, in fact, an Eaton bankruptcy. But it wasn't Timothy's. Rather it was the failure of a business that quite legitimately operated under the Eaton name on lower Yonge Street. A small gentleman's furnishings shop under the banner James Eaton and Co. and located at 86 Yonge Street (on the west side a few doors north of King) was opened by Timothy's older brother in 1882. James, two years older than Timothy, had emigrated to Upper Canada (Ontario), and during the boys' early years in the province the pair had frequently worked together. When Timothy decided on a Toronto location, James first moved to London, Ontario, but soon revised his thinking and relocated in the provincial capital city. Over the ensuing years, the James Eaton establishment unabashedly traded on the Eaton connection, much to the dismay and, following James's death, anger of Timothy. Following James's demise his son John Weldon Eaton took over. When the company failed in the summer of 1894 the new owners, Thomas Thompson and Son, kept the name Eaton on the signs and in the ads where the business was often referred to as "little Eaton's" or "Eaton's London branch" (conveniently forgetting the word *Ontario*). Rapid expansion followed, and in 1895 the James Eaton Company moved into a huge building at the corner of Yonge and Temperance streets. A devastating fire in May, 1897, destroyed the building and stock, and when the insurance company began inspecting the company books, and those of other Thompson holdings, the true nature of the so-called Eaton business came to light. Not longer after, the James Eaton Company found itself out of business. Timothy, with just a hint of a smile on his face, soldiered on.

The title of this column turned out to be a bit premature. Eaton's went out of business near the end of 1999. Several Eaton stores survive, in name at least, and are operated by Sears Canada Inc. The Eaton Centre name remains unchanged.

GONE UP IN SMOKE

March 16, 1997

Now let me get this straight. I can have a cigarette with my dinner if I'm in a restaurant on Yonge Street provided that the establishment is north of Hogg's Hollow thereby putting the place outside Toronto in a city called North York where smoking in a restaurant used to be illegal but that's another story altogether. And I can smoke like a chimney during lunch if I sit in an eatery that's on the west bank of the Humber River (another city, only this time it's called Etobicoke), but not if it's on the east bank which happens to be in Toronto. And if I sit and have a bagel and cigarette in a doughnut shop on the east side of Victoria Park Avenue I'm OK 'cause I'm in a third city, Scarborough, but if I dare try that in Country Style or Tim Horton's on the east side (back in Toronto) I'm in real trouble unless I'm on the west side of that same street north of the CNR tracks, which puts me into East York, where it's perfectly acceptable to smoke your brains out, or what, by this point in our geography lesson, part of them remains.

In 1923 cigarette and tobacco billboards cover an old building at the northeast corner of Front and York streets. A few years later the billboards as well as the structure would disappear as work began on the new Royal York Hotel.

Actually, this question, for me at least, is purely academic since I don't, nor have I ever smoked (except for a brief tussle with a pipe that nearly cost me a tooth as I looked over my left shoulder with pipe in mouth ramming same into the car window).

But the aforementioned scenario does give those dumb enough to still be smoking cause to believe in the one-unified-city concept where one unified set of by-laws will permit smokers to know they're breaking a by-law without having to resort to a map. Or what about encouraging diners to make their own choice of a smoking or nonsmoking establishment when selecting a place for breakfast, lunch, or dinner? Nah, that'll never work. It's too sensible for the butt patrol at City Hall.

The prevailing laws prohibiting tobacco advertising, cautionary warnings, Toronto's new no-smoking by-law, and pending legislation severely limiting event sponsorship by tobacco companies are certainly signs of the times and are especially intriguing when compared with times gone by when smoking was promoted and encouraged and potential health problems ignored. In fact, smoking was quite simply the thing to do. Take for instance this ad placed in a 1910 edition of the old Toronto *World* newspaper. "The man who smokes the right kind of cigarette carries in his pocket 10 aids to happiness, 10 joy riders the likes of which the non-smoker can never know. To ensure complete enjoyment of each 15 minute joy ride that a good cigarette represents smoke only Tucketts!!" In another ad, Craven A dubbed itself the "health cigarette." The Sheffield Lunch Room at Yonge and Adelaide reminded Torontonians that, "It's great to be able to smoke after your lunch without feeling you are making a nuisance of yourself. Come and bring your favourite brand, no matter how strong. You will find one worse here." Meanwhile hundreds of billboards placed on vacant buildings and hoardings around building sites all over the city silently trumpeted various brands of cigarettes and plug and cut tobaccos. Interestingly, when Queen's Park prohibited the sale of liquor in 1916, many believed that the sale of tobacco products was next on its list. Some even visualized squads of police in motor cars rushing about the city seizing tobacco where found or smelling the breath of those involved in motor collisions for the telltale odour of the pernicious tobacco weed. But it wasn't to be. In fact, in 1922 a tobacco price war broke out with United Cigar Stores, who had opened its first store at the corner of Yonge and Queen streets in 1898, dropping the price of all 15¢ packages to 12¢. There were similar reductions on more expensive brands with the premium 40¢ packages selling for just 35¢. Not to be outdone, rival Alive Bollard's, "Toronto's leading tobacconist" (strange first name for a tobacco seller it turns out), dropped the price of a pack of 20 Players to 29¢ with 30 Black Cat or Rex cigarettes selling for just 35¢. Ten Murads, Moguls, or Benson and Hedges Egyptians were 20¢.

But not everyone was happy with the ever escalating sale of tobacco products. No doubt the smoker was getting a deal as a result of the price war, but there was concern voiced for the 500 or so disabled returned veterans from the Great War who were almost totally dependant on the profits from their little smoke shops for a living. Even the Women's Christian Temperance Union got into the fray and while its members applauded the arrival of Prohibition they also felt that the annual sale of 50 billion cigarettes contributed in no small way to the ruination of the physical and moral health of the country's children. As far as they were concerned the total banning of cigarettes was long overdue. Oh, the year? 1922.

MORE CANADIAN AVIATION HISTORY

March 27, 1997

Recently, an interesting, if controversial, miniseries about the Avro Arrow was featured on CBC-TV. As spectacular as the Arrow was by the time it first flew in 1957 Avro Canada had already turned out another equally revolutionary product. In fact, whenever you hear the term *jetliner* as applied to today's modern 747s, 767s, or any jet-propelled passenger aircraft, you should remember that the word was coined specifically to describe this country's own C-102 Jetliner, North America's first jet passenger plane and second by mere weeks to the world's first, the ill-fated de Havilland Comet. The Jetliner first flew on August 10, 1949, and like its sibling would also be "shot down" by the Canadian government. Today, only a portion of the Jetliner's front fuselage remains in an Ottawa museum.

Interested in learning more about Canada's fascinating aviation history? Why not join the Toronto Chapter of the Canadian Aviation Historical Society? They have great meetings and publish a fascinating newsletter. Membership info can be obtained by writing to the Canadian Aviation Historical Society, 85 Thorncliffe Park Drive, Apartment 3710, Toronto, M4H 1L6.

Avro Jetliner

And while on the subject of Canadian transportation history, I received a letter from reader Gordon Curl, who is helping a friend from south of the border research the history of the Durant automobile factory in Leaside that turned out various products such as the Durant, Star, and Frontenac cars and Reo and Rugby trucks. The story of the complex on Laird Drive between Wicksteed and Commercial avenues is interesting and varied. The original section of the factory was erected about 1914 by Canada Wire and Cable. Here it was anticipated that the company would churn out great quantities of transmission wire necessary to bring electricity to the city from the new generating stations at the Falls. As the Great War dragged on, however, it was decided that the factory, renamed Leaside Munitions Company Limited, would first be used to aid in the war effort by turning out much needed shell casings. The plant was expanded several times, and when the war ended the property not needed by Canada Wire was taken over by the newly formed Durant Motor Car Company of Canada. The American parent company had been established by Billy Durant, who had founded General Motors in 1908 and who, after losing control of his first company, created another, Durant Motors, in 1921. At his Leaside factory thousands of Durants and Stars were produced, along with small numbers of Road King trucks. When the Durant operation in Canada failed in 1931, Dominion Motors kept the factory going with the production of the all Canadian Frontenac. Until the end of 1933, that is, when this company too went out of business. Canada Wire has recently vacated the site.

** Thanks to all who wrote with their memories of Bert's Turkey Palace (including the restaurant's manageress from 1947 to 1967), a once popular drive-in restaurant at the Richview Road and Highway 27 intersection in Etobicoke. Unfortunately, I was unable to come up with a photo of the place which is not surprising since, as many recalled, "We thought it would always be there." Turns out Bert was Bert Hedges (nearby Hedges Boulevard honours him), who was also a well-known amateur hockey official; some thought he refereed a few games in the NHL. Anyone remember Bert? Is he still with us?

** Sometime in mid-June of this year Toronto will lose another of its historic church congregations with the closing of Wesley United at Dundas and Ossington streets as a result of ever dwindling attendance figures. The original Wesley Church, with seating for 500 worshippers, opened in the summer of 1875. Attendance grew rapidly and by 1887 a new, larger church, with seating for 1 100, was ready to serve the community. It is recorded that in 1909 the membership, including that of the Sunday School (which at nearly 1 400 was the largest of all Methodist churches in the entire country), had reached nearly 3 000. In 1957 the entire complex was destroyed by a fire of unknown origins. A new Wesley United Church (which over the years has welcomed the congregations of Crawford Street, Grace-Carmen and Westmoreland churches) was dedicated on February 5, 1961. Now it, too, will close.

NATIONAL TRADE CENTRE SET TO OPEN

March 30, 1997

The new $180 million National Trade Centre.

Toronto — *It was announced today that a $45 million National Trade and Convention Centre is in the plans for the Canadian National Exhibition grounds. According to an official source the cost would be split between federal and provincial governments and metropolitan Toronto. A local architectural firm has been told to proceed with plans for the new structure which will connect with the existing Coliseum and Automotive Building.*

Actually, the mammoth project for the CNE grounds had been under discussion for months and with this news release it appeared as if the good old Exhibition was finally going to get the much needed new building. But wait a minute. What's the date of this item? Oh, here it is, on the back of the paper. What? January 27, 1967. Thirty years ago!

Now, fast forward three whole decades to the present, and in today's paper we're advised that the new National Trade Centre down at the Exhibition grounds will finally open to the public next Friday.

That's not to say that what was under discussion way back in 1967 is in reality what we're going to get. The convention centre part of that proposed complex actually opened more than a dozen years ago, but it was over on Front Street West. It's been so successful that it's now being enlarged. And as for that 1967 price tag of $45 million, that has grown to $180 million. Interestingly, though, the funding partners (technically identified as Ottawa, Queen's Park, and Metro, but in reality we the taxpayers) have remained the same.

At first glance, the new National Trade Centre (that name will no doubt change if and when a sponsor is found) could easily be mistaken for a 747 jumbo jet hangar because of its enormous size. And while it's tough to make a structure of this size look like anything but a mammoth hangar, in the case of the National Trade Centre the architects have done a particularly nice job by having the east end of the Princes' Boulevard facade mimic the classic Automotive Building across the way (to which it's connected by an underground tunnel). To the north, the interface with the Coliseum complex is accomplished via a huge covered atrium that highlights the thoughtful restoration of the Coliseum's elegant 1921 facade, which over the years has been frequently altered, and not always with a great deal of thought.

Taken in total the National Trade Centre, Automotive Building, and Coliseum complex combination at Exhibition Place features more than a million square feet of display space. The public will get to inspect Metro's newest landmark for the first time while visiting this year's Home Show.

The TTC proudly displayed its huge collection of snow-fighting equipment in front of the CNE's Electrical and Engineering Building. This building was demolished in the early 1970s and the National Trade Centre built on the site.

While the National Trade Centre arrives on the scene all bright and shiny and new, it also perpetuates the long tradition of using the Exhibition grounds as a meeting place that began in 1750 with the

French fur trading fort, Fort Rouillé. Since then 118 annual fairs and countless numbers of trade and consumer shows have been held on the grounds of Exhibition Place in buildings such as the spectacular Crystal Palace, the Governments Building, the Transportation Building, the Ontario Building, the Manufacturers Building, the Electrical and Engineering Building, Queen Elizabeth Building and, of course, the newly rejuvenated Coliseum complex and Automotive Building. The new National Trade Centre will join this remarkable inventory of buildings.

** New from the Ontario Heritage Foundation is a fascinating and entertaining publication titled Ontario's Heritage, *A Celebration of Conservation*. Highlighted in the book are many of the natural, manmade, and cultural heritage sites throughout the province that were identified and, in many cases, preserved for future generations during the foundation's first 30 years. The book is available at the Ontario Heritage Centre, 10 Adelaide Street East, and at the gift shop in the Elgin and Winter Garden Theatre Centre opposite the Eaton Centre.

A PIECE OF HISTORY IS ON THE MOVE

April 6, 1997

Every so often an anniversary pops up that truly makes you realize time is flying by. One such revelation was presented to me several weeks ago, and if I hadn't had a calculator if front of me at that moment I would never have believed that Campbell House (which for many people has always stood at the northwest corner of Queen Street and University Avenue) was moved to that location exactly a quarter of century ago.

Campbell House is winched from Adelaide Street onto University Avenue. Note gravel trucks farther up the street acting as anchor points, March 31, 1972.

And the gentleman who jogged my memory was certainly the person who should know, for it was Vim Kochar who, along with the late Harvey Self, supervised, free of charge, the remarkable feat of moving the 300-ton structure from its original location on Adelaide Street East, at the top of Frederick Street, a total of 5 305 feet to its new home at Queen and University.

Actually the rescue operation began months before when the Advocate Society, an association of trial lawyers, learned that old house, which had been erected in 1822 as a residence for one of the first members of Toronto's legal profession, was scheduled for demolition. Fortunately, the owners of the house, which, since Campbell's wife's death in 1844, had been used for various purposes including as a factory and a warehouse, offered to donate the building to anyone on the condition that the structure be removed from the site.

Enter the Advocate Society who, along with the newly created Sir William Campbell Foundation, arranged to have the structure moved to a location donated by the Canada Life Assurance Company (currently celebrating its 150th anniversary). That history-making, as well as history-saving, move took place exactly 25 years ago.

Starting at daybreak on March 31, 1972, the old house, which had earlier been jacked up to free it from the original foundation and placed on six dollies made up of a total of 56 rubber-tired wheels, was winched off the site where it had sat for a century and a half and out onto Adelaide Street to begin its unusual journey. The move would be accomplished by carefully winching the building forward short distances using two large trucks filled with gravel as anchor points. The trucks would then move ahead a short distance, and the winching operation was repeated.

The route selected for the move, west on Adelaide (albeit the wrong way on the one-way eastbound street) and north on University Avenue to a site opposite the south lawn of the Canada Life property, was chosen over other routes primarily because the streetcar tracks on Adelaide had been constructed years ago so that they would easily support the weight of two passing cars. Nevertheless, employees of various civic departments as well as a few from Bell Telephone were kept busy shoring up 65 manholes, temporarily removing miles of overhead wire, 82 street lights, two utility poles, and several traffic lights. An alternate route via Frederick, Front, and University was rejected primarily because of the city's huge underground parking garage beneath University Avenue north of Front.

Chief Justice Sir William Campbell's residence in its original location on Adelaide Street East (originally Duke Street), 1970.

Campbell House at its new address on Queen Street West at University where tours are conducted and the story of the move told daily.

Toronto Sketches 6

Tens of thousands of sidewalk superintendents (each with a camera) watched the procession that took six hours to get to University and Queen. Then, deteriorating weather conditions resulted in the building resting overnight straddling the southbound lanes of University Avenue. The operation concluded the following morning when the house was moved onto its new site virtually none the worse for wear.

PLAYIN' BALL WITH CUBA

April 13, 1997

Maple Leaf Stadium at the southwest corner of Lake Shore Blvd. W. and Bathurst Street in the late 1950s.

"*Vamos a commenzar el juego!*" (Translation: Play ball!)

W ith those words, Toronto's baseball season got under way in Havana, Cuba, exactly 38 years ago tomorrow.

It was the opening of the 1959 season for the Toronto Maple Leaf team of the Triple A International League back in 1959. That league was one step below the majors, and had been established in the closing years of the last century.

Toronto's entry into this predominantly American association was only natural. The city's been a hotbed of baseball interest ever since our boys first began playing ball in the old Sunlight Stadium, just steps away from Queen and Broadview.

For many years, the league was barely international — the only two teams from outside the U.S. were from Toronto and Montreal. Then in 1954, Cuba joined the league with a team called the Sugar Kings.

But as conditions in Cuba under president Fulgencio Batista deteriorated and bullets and bombs began to fly, crowds that showed up to watch the team play at Havana's Grand Stadium dwindled to less than 1 500 jittery fans.

Newspaper ad for the Toronto-Havana baseball game, April 14, 1959.

With Castro's eventual overthrow of the Batista government in early 1959, things began to look up, on the ball field at least. Interestingly, one reason for optimism on the Cuban baseball front was the signing of a half dozen American born players. Unfortunately for Cuba, the outcome of that opening game on April 14, 1959, was less than inspiring, even though Fidel did throw out the first ball. Our guys won 6 to 4 on Cuban born Hector Rodriquez's pinch-hit homer in the 11th. Anyone seen Hector?

Later that month, Havana arrived in Toronto for the local home opener. The reception committee expected that Cuba's new president would honour the city by again throwing out the first ball. This time, however, Fidel was busy elsewhere. Nevertheless, "Honest Ed" Mirvish showed up and presented Capt. F. Guerra, the country's sports director, with a new tractor for the people of Cuba.

A young Fidel Castro.

A TASTE OF THE TITANIC: Exactly 85 years ago tomorrow evening, the passenger ship RMS *Titanic* sideswiped an iceberg in the North Atlantic. Few of the hundreds of passengers - including many from Toronto — who were enjoying dinner that Sunday evening felt the vessel shudder as the giant liner suffered a mortal wound.

Within two hours the *Titanic* was no more. The sinking wasn't the worst sea disaster in history (1 513 crew and passengers perished), but it has become the best known. Now this may be a strange question, but have you ever wondered what was on the menu that last night on board the great ship?

A new book, *Last Dinner on the Titanic* (Hyperion/Madison Press, $33.95), takes the reader into *Titanic's* kitchens and dining rooms that fateful evening. There's even a selection of recipes so you can create your *Titanic* soirée. Incidentally, Madison Press is a

Toronto publisher which has also been responsible for Bob Ballard's *Discovery of the Titanic* — arguably the definitive book about this legendary ship — and many other books that have become international bestsellers.

SUNNYBROOK ESTABLISHED TO HEAL WAR'S WOUNDED

April 20, 1997

As the Ontario government goes about the unpleasant task ofclosing hospitals, it's interesting to return to a time whenfederal, provincial, and municipal officials anxiously awaitedthe opening of a much needed and long overdue hospital onToronto's northern outskirts. Sunnybrook Hospital, one ofMetro's largest and busiest medical facilities, had its originsduring the early years of the Second World War when theever-increasing numbers of wounded returning from overseas beganto overwhelm the nation's existing public and veterans'hospitals.

The Christie Street Hospital was built as the National Cash Register factory. This view, years after its conversion to a hospital, was taken in 1928.

Here in Toronto, the Military Orthopaedic Hospital, located onthe west side of Christie Street adjacent to the noisy CPR railwayline and just north of Dupont Street (most people simplyreferred to it as the Christie Street hospital), had become thecountry's principal treatment facility for First World War veterans.It had been established in 1918, when a cash registerfactory was turned into a hospital by removing manufacturingequipment and building a series of wards, a few operatingtheatres, and a few other necessities found in hospitals.After the Great War, it continued to be used as an active,400-bed convalescent military hospital.

The first patient to be admitted to the new hospital was Private Raymond Scott, seen here with nurse Mary Sissen as he gets ready to leave old Christie Street Hospital.

When the next world war erupted in 1939, officials assumed thatthe Christie Street hospital would simply go on serving more woundedservicemen. However, as the war progressed and the numbers of woundedcontinued to grow, it became painfully obvious that something had to be done to increase the old hospital's ability to cope.

At first, the federal government was convinced that by simplyenlarging the old building to an 800-bed facility the problemwould be solved. Officials were unprepared for the public outcryand denunciation of this simplistic approach to a condition thathad become a national emergency.Fortunately, a number of public-spirited citizens, including

Lady Eaton, wife of businessman Sir John Eaton, who had done muchto aid his country during the Great War, took up thechallenge. This group insisted that a proper veterans' hospitalbe constructed. It would have a single purpose — to administerto the medical needs of those who had been disabled, physicallyor mentally, while fighting to keep Canada free.

Formal opening ceremonies at the new Sunnybrook Military Hospital, June 12, 1948.

The majority of citizens believed that the creation of a modernveterans' hospital was the least the nation could do to show itsappreciation, and this overwhelming public opinion quicklyconvinced the government that a new facility was necessary. But where could it be built? Toronto had the answer, Sunnybrook Park.This 175-acre park, originally owned by prominent Torontobusinessman Joseph Kilgour and called Sunnybrook Farm, had beendeeded to the City of Toronto by Kilgour'swidow, Alice, soon after her husband's death in 1925.

During the official dedication of the park on September 13, 1928Mayor Sam McBride stated, "In the minds of the thousands who will visit Toronto's newest park, Sunnybrook will remain a fitting and lasting memorial to Joseph Kilgour, a man who helped build up the city in which he carried on business for many years." However, the park's beautiful location well outside the city'snorthern boundary was to create a major problem for the manyTorontonians who were without cars and found visiting their new park difficult. Eventually, the TTC added a suburban bus routeto serve the new Sunnybrook Park.

A few years later, not long after the outbreak of the SecondWorld War, government officials began looking for a site for a newnational military hospital. It was Toronto's mayor Dr. FrederickConboy (he was a dentist) who suggested that Sunnybrook Parkmight be appropriate. But first, the heirs to the Kilgour estatehad to release the city from its obligation to keep the propertyopen as a public park. Getting the heirs to agree with the concept of a portion of thepark being used as a hospital site was the easy part;construction of that hospital was much more difficult. The actual sod-turning didn't take place until Remembrance Day,1943, and the cornerstone wasn't laid until the year after that.

The ongoing delays were caused by the scarcity of building materials, lack of both skilled and unskilled labour, and a succession of strikes. And while a few patients were admitted in the fall of 1946, it wasn't until June 12, 1948, four years after the first sod was turned, that Prime Minister Mackenzie King was to officially open the new $10-million Sunnybrook Military Hospital.

In 1966, ownership of land and facilities was transferred by thefederal government to the University of Toronto. In 1990 the facility was given its present title, Sunnybrook Health Sciences Centre. Major additions and improvements continue to be made to this world-famous hospital.

A GALLANT SHIP REMEMBERED

April 27, 1997

The navy's new HMCS *Shawinigan*, scheduled to be commissioned
June 16, 1997.

I recently received a note from reader Jim McAlister advising that the Canadian navy's new Maritime Coastal Defence Vessel (MCDV) HMCS *Shawinigan* is to be commissioned this coming June 16 at Trois Rivières, Quebec. And while at first glance this may not appear to be a story of local importance, a closer look reveals that an earlier HMCS *Shawinigan*, a Second World War corvette, did indeed have a very close, and sad, connection with Toronto. And it's the original *Shawinigan*'s fate that has naval officials looking for relatives of its crew members in hopes that they might attend the ceremony. Here's the story.

As the idea that war with the Third Reich was inevitable, members of the British Admiralty began to examine plans for the production of a close escort vessel for use in the country's coastal waters. What materialized was something called Patrol Vessel, Whaler Type, a 205-foot-long craft with a 33-foot beam and drawing 15 feet of water that was based on the *Southern Pride*, a whaling vessel built at the English shipyard of Smith's Dock Company at Southbank on Tees.

Here in Canada, officials were seeking ways to help the war effort. One idea was to build vessels for the navy in the country's various shipyards However, since most of these yards had no experience building large ships, it was decided that Canada would manufacture the smaller corvettes and minesweepers. One of these feisty little craft, HMCS *Shawinigan*, a corvette produced in the Davie shipyard in Lauzon, Quebec (now Canada's oldest and largest shipyard) flying the pendant K-136, was commissioned on September 19, 1941, at Quebec City. Early in the war *Shawinigan* provided escort coverage for three cross-Atlantic convoys, St. John's, Newfoundland, to Londonderry, and in June of 1942 was reassigned to Quebec and Labrador convoy duty. Over the next two years she faithfully carried out a variety of assignments. On November 25, 1944, while conducting an independent antisubmarine patrol in the Cabot Strait, *Shawinigan* was torpedoed by U 1228. The attack was quick and deadly. No distress messages were ever received and *Shawinigan* sank with all hands.

The ill-fated HMCS *Shawinigan*, sunk with all hands, November 25, 1944.

While researching this article I examined copies of the Toronto *Evening Telegram* newspaper kept on file in the *Sun* library. While we now know that the tragedy occurred on November 25, wartime censorship kept any references to the event out of the paper until December 7, 1944, when that day's edition featured a brief front page story headlined "Sea Veteran Ship Lost In Atlantic." The story goes on to describe the loss of the ship, although at the time the cause of the sinking was unknown. We now know that among the 94 officers and ratings lost on that cold November day were nearly three dozen from Ontario, a figure that included twelve from the Toronto area: Dudley

Garrett, Gordon Brown, Alfred Clayton, Harry Cole, Robert Grant, Harold Hurd, Arthur Kemp, Leslie Langfeld, Michael O'Gorman, Clifford Rea, Gilbert Vincent, and Wilfred Watson. The next of kin of these gallant sailors are invited to attend the commissioning of the new HMCS *Shawinigan* in mid-June.

A GIFTED FUNNYMAN

May 4, 1997

While I've been unable to calculate just how many times Victor Borge has been a guest in our city, that number has to be considerable when one realizes that his first Toronto visit was more than a half century ago.

Victor Borge

When Victor arrived in Toronto in 1943 to join other stars performing in a war bond concert at Massey Hall, the Allies were being pounded on all fronts. Years later Borge revealed in a newspaper article that he was pretty sure Toronto was, if not *the* first, certainly one of the first cities in which he had ever performed a solo concert. "And that's why it's not difficult to understand why I just love Toronto," he added.

Borge was born in Copenhagen, Denmark, in 1909 and came by his appreciation for music honestly. Victor's father was a talented violinist with the Royal Danish Philharmonic Orchestra, but it was his mother who got the youngster started on the piano. That's because "my father kept hoggin' the violin," Borge later disclosed.

For the youngster piano practice was a true ordeal. Nevertheless, he persevered and after years of hard work Victor finally made his concert debut. He was eight.

At first the youngster performed his programs of complicated concert pieces with sincerity and seriousness. Then one evening, while deeply immersed in Rachmaninoff's "Second Piano Concerto," Victor stepped out of character. Noticing that the orchestra had speeded up, leaving the 14-year-old well behind, the youngster suddenly stopped playing, walked over to the conductor and pointed to notes on the score announcing in no uncertain terms that this is where he was and not over there where the conductor and the rest of the orchestra thought he should be. Turning to an astonished audience, Victor flashed a quick wink and returned to the piano bench. His totally unexpected performance brought down the house. The Borge style had shown itself.

Torontonians loved Borge during his visits to the Casino Theatre on Queen Street West in 1950 and 1951. The little Casino, one of the city's true landmark theatres, was located where the Sheraton Centre stands today.

With the unwelcome arrival of the Nazis in his homeland some years later, Victor prudently decided to move to the United States where he eventually got work as a warm-up pianist entertaining audiences eagerly awaiting the start of one the numerous live radio shows. While the job did afford Victor a taste of show business, he was really just background. His first real break came with a guest appearance on the

Bing Crosby Kraft Music Hall, one of the network's most popular shows. Victor was such a hit he remained a guest for more than a year.

Over the next few years Borge performed throughout the States, finally making a return visit to Toronto in the summer of 1950. This time, rather than being just part of the show as he had been during his 1943 Massey Hall war bond visit, Borge *was* the show. He had been booked into Toronto's Casino Theatre on the south side of Queen Street opposite today's new City Hall, which had originally opened in 1936 as a vaudeville house. In the early 1950s the theatre's entertainment policy changed and soon up and coming (and still inexpensive) young talent, people like Tony Bennett, Vic Damone, Mel Tormé, Henny Youngman, Guy Mitchell, Kay Starr, the Four Lads, and such big-band icons-to-be as Louis Armstrong, Count Basie, Dizzie Gillespie, Cab Calloway, and even the Dorsey Brothers were being featured.

Joining this list of future stars was young Victor Borge, who even then was trumpeted in a series of newspaper ads as "the one and only Victor Borge, world famous wit and wizard of the piano." And just in case that 75¢ admission fee seemed a little stiff, the night's entertainment also included comedian Lou Nelson, juggler Larry Weeks, dancing sensations the Gregory Girls and "your singing MC" Bob Goodman. And there was a movie, something called *The Mutineers*, which may have just been bad enough to clear the house so another crowd could be shoehorned in.

But the reviews were all positive with the *Telegram*'s Clem Shields completely taken with something Borge did that the pianist termed "inflationary language," you know, "elevennis, anytwo?"

Borge returned to the Casino again the next year, but by 1953 had graduated to a stage in the mammoth Maple Leaf Gardens where he was the hit of that year's Easter Seal Show. Torontonians still hadn't had enough, and later that same year Borge returned to star at that year's Canadian National Exhibition. In 1957 he returned to the intimacy of the Massey Hall stage and in 1960 was a sensation at the CNE Grandstand once again. In 1962 O'Keefe Centre audiences loudly cheered the great Dane while in 1965 a well-publicized tiff with CNE Grandstand show producer Jack Arthur filled the newspapers as well as (and perhaps not totally by coincidence) the Grandstand seats.

In the years that followed Victor has been with us on numerous occasions. Interestingly, next Saturday's visit will see Victor back on the same stage on which he introduced Torontonians to the Borge magic exactly 54 years ago. Welcome home, Victor.

WILL IT ARRIVE ON TIME?

May 11, 1997

I've been following the proposal to build a new Maple Leaf Gardens over the train sheds south of Union Station with great interest. Unfortunately, as I sit here writing this column well in advance of its publication date, I have no way of knowing whether it'll ever happen. Even as I type, the latest word is that both the Leafs and Raptors are discussing the possibility of moving into the structure. What they'll do to the old Postal Delivery Building is a bit of a mystery.

However, as much as I think the idea of a new Gardens over the station train sheds is a great one, my hope is that they're able to get the doors to the place open in less time than it took to build the train sheds in the first place.

In the old photo accompanying this article we can see the sheds under construction in June of 1927. They are connected to the new (and when this photo was taken still unopened) Union Station, while the tower of the city's old Union Station, on the south side of Front Street west of York, looms in the foreground. The new Gardens, if the proposal goes through, will sit on top of the sheds through which the trains continue to operate, though in numbers far fewer than those experienced in the 1930s and 1940s.

My cynicism about whether the new building will be up and running in less time than it took to get the train sheds operational is based on the fact that a full quarter century passed between the time they were first proposed as part of the cross-waterfront railway viaduct project and the day the sheds became operational.

The railway viaduct had been visualized as the answer to the problem of the city being cut off from its waterfront by railway tracks, the first pair of which had been laid down in 1853. This impediment was not only annoying, it was also dangerous. As the freight and passenger train traffic in and out of the old railway station on the south side of Front Street west of York increased, more and more often the wagons and pedestrians attempting to use the city's major north-south downtown streets would be brought to a standstill. On occasion, some who had lost patience at the blocked crossing would attempt to crawl under the stationary

Work progresses on the train sheds south of Toronto's new Union Station in June 1927. The rail lines to the right of the photo would eventually be realigned onto the newly constructed elevated viaduct and run into the new station through the sheds.

box or baggage cars. More than a few times the shunting would resume at precisely the wrong moment with disastrous results.

As early as 1905 city and railway officials agreed to do something about the problem, which could not be allowed to persist, not if the city was to continue to grow. And while everyone seemed to appreciate the seriousness of the situation, each time work was ready to begin the railways would come up with another obstacle that would stall the project once again. This went on for a several years, and it wasn't until 1909 that government authorities finally stepped in and insisted that a new station be built. It would be served by through tracks laid on an elevated viaduct that would allow some, but not all, north-south thoroughfares in the downtown area to run unhindered under the tracks. Incidentally, the term *union station* was selected since the building was to be used by a union of the two railways serving Toronto, the Grand Trunk and Canadian Pacific, although by the time the station finally opened the first would be part of the newly established Canadian National Railways, along with a third transcontinental line, Sir William Mackenzie's Canadian Northern, which reached the city in 1905.

An integral part of the routing over the new viaduct was specially designed train sheds equipped with state-of-the-art overhead exhaust vents to dispel the belching smoke from the numerous steam engines that would chug in and out of the station by the dozens every day. Passengers were able to use the new Union Station in the summer of 1927. It would be another two years before the viaduct, complete with train sheds, would be ready for train traffic.

So as I said, they've got from now until 2021 to build the new Gardens over the train sheds if they want to do it in less time than it took to build those same sheds.

On June 24, 1997, Toronto City Council rejected an offer of $34 million for lease rights to build a new $300-million stadium over Union Station. The city said those rights were worth at least $100 million. The Leafs wouldn't budge, and the intriguing proposal was derailed. Alternate sites, such as Exhibition Place, Downsview Airport, Moss Park Armoury, and lands west of SkyDome were examined before the Leafs bought the Toronto Raptors and the two teams built the Air Canada Centre.

HOW SUNDAY STREETCAR SERVICE GOT ON TRACK

May 18, 1997

With all the hustle and bustle we experience here in our big city every day of the week, it's difficult to imagine that there was a time when even the idea of riding a streetcar on a Sunday was considered an act of sacrilege. Sure, you could ride the horse-drawn cars of the Toronto Street Railway Company, and later the electric vehicles of the Toronto Railway Company, Monday through Saturday, but come Sunday, the use of this form of public transportation was a definite no-no. Unless you were a can of milk, that is, or some other farm produce. Those important commodities were allowed to be transported by rail into the city from any of the farms that surrounded Toronto in the late 1800s even on Sunday.

It wasn't until May 23, 1897, exactly 100 years ago this coming Friday, that the ban on Sunday streetcar operation was lifted. Effective that day, you could even go to church on the streetcar.

To understand why there was such opposition to the operation of public transit vehicles on the Sabbath (back then in Toronto there were only streetcars, no buses, no subways), one has to forget the cosmopolitan nature of our modern city. The Christian church — especially the Church of England and the Methodist faiths — was all-powerful, and a quite literal translation of the *dos* and *don't*s spelled out in the Bible was the rule, a rule unquestioned. And so when the clergy spoke from the city's numerous pulpits, the vast majority of Torontonians listened and obeyed. Frequent references to the sorry state of affairs in American cities like Chicago and New York were brought forth as an example of what could happen to a community when the devil gets his (or is it her?) way and the streetcars are allowed to operate on the Sabbath. That, plus the fact that the owner of the country's largest bicycle manufacturing concern, a form of public transportation that stood to lose big time if the streetcars were given a seven-day green light, was a confirmed Methodist. Hart Almerin Massey gave the opponents to Sunday operation a highly visible and vocal say about how things should continue to unfold in Toronto the good.

The financial barons around town who had vested financial interests in the transportation system, people like William Mackenzie (who owned the street railway company), Henry Mill Pellatt (who owned the company that generated the electricity), and Billy Maclean (whose newspaper, the *World*, made more than a few dollars on the ads and notices placed therein promoting Sunday operation), fought the so-called "good guys" only to be defeated in the plebiscites held in 1892 and again in 1893. But with the number of voters rejecting Sunday operation much lower after the 1893 vote (1892: 3 936 against, 1893: 973 against) the swing in the mood of Torontonians was becoming obvious.

The status quo was maintained for the next few years before the yes side determined the time was opportune to try again. The arguments, pro and con, were essentially carry-overs from the previous campaigns. One interesting change was a letter in the *Globe* newspaper that, in effect, refuted the claim that Sunday streetcars would ruin the morals and reputation enjoyed in Toronto the good. The author of the letter concluded, after touring various American communities such as Providence, Detroit, Cleveland, and Buffalo, where Sunday operation had been accepted, and then interviewing citizens and clergy alike, that Sunday cars did not bring on "drunkenness, vice and beer gardens." On the contrary. The author had met orderly, sober, and happy crowds, and as one minister had confided, the Sunday streetcars had become a great boon to churchgoers. Whether the writer's expenses were covered by one or other of the sides was not revealed.

Back in Toronto, meetings were held (the anticar forces congregating in the newly constructed Massey Hall, the procar people in the Auditorium on Queen Street just east of City Hall) and parades wound through the downtown streets. This time the plight of the poor working masses seemed to get more attention. Why should the rich be able to get to and fro in their fancy carriages on Sunday while the less well-off (including the carriage drivers, footmen, and servants of those same well-heeled Torontonians) have to stay at home because the operation of public transportation vehicles was prohibited on Sunday?

The Sunday car question was put to the electorate once again on May 15, 1897, and this time seven-day street railway service was approved, but only by a slim majority, 16 273 votes to 16 051. Thus, as a result of a plurality of a mere 321 votes Torontonians were granted the right to ride a streetcar on Sunday. Service began May 23, 1897, exactly 100 years ago this coming Friday.

But as pointed out by Christopher Armstrong and H.V. Nelles in their book *The Revenge of the Methodist Bicycle Company* (Peter

Martin and Associates, 1977), the same bicycle manufacturers who had fought Sunday streetcar service (for whatever reason) could take some measure of solace, as an unforseen bicycle craze began to sweep the nation.

As hundreds of bicycle riders swept past half-deserted streetcars on those warm summer Sundays in 1897, the railway barons' dreams of huge profits failed to materialize. Yes, the Methodist bicycle company had its revenge.

As strange as it may seem, there was a time when Torontonians couldn't go to church by streetcar on Sunday. That all changed exactly 100 years ago next Friday. This view shows a horse-drawn streetcar in front of St. Andrew's Presbyterian Church, King and Simcoe streets, c. 1880.

MOVING AHEAD WITH GO

May 25, 1997

In a 1919 photo, the radial cars connecting Sunnyside (in the distance) and Port Credit are seen running adjacent to the original Toronto to Hamilton highway at the entrance to High Park (now Colborne Lodge Drive). The site of the future GO train right-of-way is at the left of the view.

The year 1967 was a special one for Canada and Canadians. The year marked the centennial of the confederation of the nation's original four provinces, Ontario, Quebec, Nova Scotia, and New Brunswick, and to celebrate many will remember attending an event that, though officially known as the Universal and International Exhibition, was known far and wide simply as Expo '67. Held on Montreal's Ile Ste-Hélène and adjacent man-made land in the St. Lawrence River, Expo '67 was a $283-million, 183-day-long blow-out that attracted more than 50 million many of whom, I'll bet, are reading this column. Those that did will no doubt find it hard to believe that the happy event opened an incredible 30 years ago last April 28.

There was another moving event (pun intended) that also got up and running 30 years ago, Ontario's innovative inter-city commuter service, GO Transit. (Incidentally, many visitors to our city are surprised when they learn the word GO actually stands for Government of Ontario.) The concept of a rail commuter service came out of an extensive transportation study into the future needs of

Metropolitan Toronto and surrounding regions, initiated by the government in 1962. Fifteen different routes were examined, and it was concluded that the lakeshore communities east and west of Toronto would be the first to be served by a new commuter rail service that would utilize trackage owned by Canadian National Railways. Heeding the recommendations of the government-sponsored study, GO Transit came into being in 1965, and work soon began on the development of the first routes, Oakville to Toronto and Pickering to Toronto.

At the start of GO Transit operations 30 years ago, the city skyline was much more modest, with the first tower of the TD Centre bracketed by the 1929 Royal York Hotel and the 1930 Bank of Commerce. Note also the O'Keefe Centre had not yet gone to the (Humming)birds. (Photo courtesy GO Transit).

The distinction of being designated the first GO train goes to train #946, which departed the Oakville station, eastbound for Toronto, at exactly 0550 hours on Tuesday, May 23, 1967. Officiating at the historic event, which took place exactly 30 years ago last Friday, May 23, 1967, was Ontario Premier John Robarts, whose government had initiated the commuter study five years before. Robarts, a enthusiastic and loyal Canadian and a man of vision, served as premier from 1961 until 1971. Sadly, after suffering several crippling strokes he took his own life in the autumn of 1982.

CN CANADIAN NATIONAL RAILWAYS CN-714 10-62

FORM 19X

TRAIN ORDER ___GO·1___

May 23 ___19__ 67__

TO	AT
Prime Minister John P. Robarts, Q.C. Province of Ontario.	OAKVILLE, Ontario (Mile 21.4)

All conditions of the Uniform Code of Operating Rules which govern Canadian railways have been met in connection with the GO Transit commuter system which covers 60.2 miles of CN track along the lakeshore corridor.

Operating Bulletin # 916 governing the movement of GO Transit Train Schedules is hereby declared operative. You may proceed on the first rush-hour train # 946 departing Oakville 0550 hours, arriving Toronto Union 0627.

All other GO Transit trains will run according to Operating Bulletin 916.

MADE __May 23__ TIME __0545__ OPR _[signature]_

Douglas V. Gonder, Vice-President
Canadian National, Toronto, Ontario

GO Transit's first train order, May 23, 1967.

Officials anticipated that the new transit service would attract 15 000 passengers a day after two years of operation. However, the system's unexpected popularity resulted in that forecast being achieved in a mere six months. Today, GO Transit carries approximately 124 000 riders each weekday with an annual ridership figure an astounding 34 million.

In the three decades that have gone by since train #946 left Oakville for Union Station remarkable changes have occurred not only throughout the Greater Toronto Area (GTA) but in the list of routes and services provided by the dedicated men and women of GO Transit. For transit history trivia buffs, here's a brief summary of GO service introductions. First regular bus route — September 8, 1970. Rail service to Georgetown — April, 1974. To Richmond Hill — May, 1978. To Milton — October, 1981. To Stouffville and Bradford — September, 1982. To Whitby from Pickering — December, 1988. To Burlington from Oakville — May, 1992. The first bi-level coaches were introduced in March, 1978, with the last of the single-level units retired in November, 1989. And we mustn't forget the major multimillion-dollar upgrading of Toronto's historic Union Station, which was undertaken by GO Transit in the late 1970s.

As with most innovations, a diligent search frequently reveals that such supposedly new events can trace their genesis to sometime in the past. While this concept could fill a dozen columns, for the moment let's focus on GO's pioneer commuter service between Toronto and Oakville. While electric interurban streetcars (known as radials in Ontario) running west from Toronto never connected with Oakville, the plan to do so was on the books in the early years of the century. Initial steps in that direction were taken with the formation of the Toronto and Mimico Railway and Light Company in 1890, which began operations from Sunnyside to the Humber River in 1892, to Mimico Creek the following year, to Long Branch in 1894, and eventually on to Port Credit in 1905. In that same year surveyors began laying out the extension to Oakville on paper, but nothing came of that plan. Sixty-two years went by, and finally on May 23, 1967, 30 years ago last Friday, GO train #946 pulled out of the Oakville station to fulfil the original ambition.

June 1, 1997

Ad for the new Toronto to Buffalo airline service to be inaugurated June 29, 1929.

Flying to the four corners of the world has become a regular occurrence, so much so that seldom do we look skyward even when one of those giant 747s crawls across the sky. But that certainly wasn't the case when the city's first regular airline passenger service was inaugurated nearly 70 years ago. With the arrival of the latest wonder of the age, the passenger plane, Toronto itself had arrived!

Flights in and out Toronto's new Port George VI Island Airport (renamed Toronto City Centre) were still eight years in the future (and the opening of a standby facility out in the countryside near the tiny community of Malton nine years away) when the city's pioneer passenger service was inaugurated by Canadian Colonial Airways Ltd. on June 29, 1929. Canadian Colonial was a subsidiary of the American Colonial Airways company, which held the distinction of being the first airline to actively promote its service to the general public rather than to simply fly the mail for the U.S. Postal Service. One year later Colonial became part of the new American Airways, renamed American Airlines in 1934.

One of Colonial Airways' pair of Sikorsky S-38s on the Toronto to Buffalo run rolls up the ramp onto dry land after landing on Toronto Bay.

Toronto's airport for the historic event was actually Toronto Bay, since the aircraft in service was a giant twin-engine Sikorsky S-38 amphibian that would land on water, then roll up a ramp onto dry land to load and unload passengers. Here in Toronto that ramp was on the edge of the bay just east of the foot of Yonge Street. With the acres and acres of landfilling that's gone on over the decades, the terminal, called the Toronto Air Harbour, would have been located just south of today's Hummingbird (O'Keefe) Centre.

Colonial entered the Toronto history books that day in June, 1929, with the inauguration of twice daily flights across Lake Ontario to Buffalo, New York, where the eight passengers could board flights connecting with numerous other communities throughout the United States and eventually to destinations worldwide.

On that first day, however, an operational problem with the ramp at the Marine Airport located at the foot of Georgia Street in Buffalo forced the landing to be made on dry land at the Greater Buffalo Airport.

Incidentally, that first southbound flight lasted all of 37 minutes, with the return trip taking 9 minutes longer due to strong north winds.

* Just in time for those of us who look forward to summer drives around our beautiful province are a couple of books, both from University of Toronto Press. The first, *Looking for Old Ontario* ($19.95) by Erindale College associate professor Thomas McIlwraith, guides us along Ontario's infrequently travelled back roads that connect the province's numerous towns and hamlets with the rest of the bustling world. The author's insightful and easily read text, supplemented by dozens of photos, sketches, and maps, helps the reader date old houses, interpret social status through graveyard architecture, and discover important buildings hidden behind modern facades on the numerous Main Streets scattered throughout the province. In general, McIlwraith's book helps all of us better appreciate life off the beaten track.

The perfect companion book is Alan Rayburn's *Place Names of Ontario* ($21.95). Just as old photographs and well researched text can provide insight into a community's past, so too can the origin of that community's name. In some cases pioneer settlers gave a hamlet its identifying moniker, for example Jackson's Point on Lake Simcoe after John Mills Jackson, or perhaps the name resulted from some prominent landscape feature, for example Forest Hill in Metro Toronto). Or perhaps it's a made-up name like Kenora, which is taken from the first two letters of a trio of neighbouring communities: Keewatin, Norman, and Rat Portage. In the book Rayburn acquaints us with the origins of 2 285 place names scattered throughout Ontario. Fascinating reading!

** With all the building activity going on in the Woodbridge area readers in that part of the world be will interested to learn that the pretty little house at 7365 Martin Grove Road (in amongst the trees on the east side of the street between Steeles Avenue and Highway 7) is going to be around for some years to come. Built in 1899 (coincidentally, the same year as Toronto's old City Hall opened) by John Johnston, the son of David Johnston, a pioneer settler in the district, the house will soon be moved a short distance to accommodate the construction of a new 123-unit condominium. Following the move the house will be made ready to begin its new life as a community centre for senior citizens and other nonprofit organizations. The work is being undertaken by the Canadian Seniors Development Corporation.

TIDY'S REMAINS A THRIVING ENTERPRISE

June 8, 1997

I'm always fascinated by long-time businesses that carry the name of the company founder. Though their numbers are dwindling (Aikenhead has vanished, as has Simpson's), a number are still around. Companies such as Eatons, Loblaws, Zellers, and Dempsters all remind us that at one time there in fact was a Timothy Eaton, a Theodore Loblaw, a Walter Zeller, and a James Dempster.

And then there's Tidy's, a name that's been associated with the retail florist business in this city for an incredible 120 years. In fact, that name recognizes Stephen Tidy, a professional gardener who arrived in Toronto from Rochester, England, in 1873 and who, after operating a small greenhouse on Ontario Street in the northern reaches of a very much smaller city, decided to try his luck in the retail flower business. Enlisting the help of his three sons, Stephen opened a small store at 47 King Street West in 1877.

Following the death of the founder in 1896, son Charles, who had gone into the rose-growing business on Bleecker Street, took over and eventually opened a new Tidy store further west on King at number 75. In 1913 another move saw the store at 79 King Street West, where the Tidy sign remained until 1964, when construction of the new Toronto Dominion Centre forced the company to move to its present location, at 526 Richmond Street East, with a second retail outlet located on the concourse level of Commerce Court just steps away from the site of the original King Street store.

Charles Tidy remained at the helm for almost half a century, and on his death in 1947 his son, Philip, took the reins, allowing the company to continue operating with a Tidy in the front office. However, in 1948 the city's oldest retail florist business, while retaining the family name, was no longer owned by the Tidy family. But if the new owner couldn't be a Tidy the business got the next best thing. Elliot Lye had joined the firm as a delivery boy in 1910 and could frequently be seen laden down with baskets or bouquets of flowers (or both) as he peddled his bicycle to the office or residence of another long-time Tidy customer.

Some years later the delivery part of the business was modernized with the acquisition of an American Austin van. The little vehicle quickly became quite a site around town, zipping in and out of traffic much like the bicycle couriers do today. The car was described as "the bantam car, smart as a new hat, thrifty as a housewife." Newspaper ads, placed by the Moore and Hughes dealership at 1009 Bay Street, assured potential buyers that the American Austin, which sold for $595, would get 48 miles to the gallon of gas, 20 000 to 40 000 miles on a set of tires, and could reach 50 miles an hour. "Visit our dealership and bring prejudices with you!!"

Keeping it all in the family, as the Tidys did, Elliot Lye's son Nick took over in 1964 with his children, Janet and Jim, assuming management duties in recent years. Tidy's, 120 years and still growing.

Tidy's Flowers at 79 King Street West. This building was demolished in the mid-1960s to permit construction of Toronto's first modern skyscraper, the TD Centre.

Once a familiar sight around downtown, Tidy's diminutive American Austin delivery van sold for around $600 back in 1930.

A GIFTED ENTERTAINER

June 15, 1997

Throughout the 1920s and 1930s one of the most frequently heard expressions was, "Al Jolson is the greatest entertainer in the whole world." And the person who most often spoke those words? Al Jolson himself. Al's show business career actually started soon after the family emigrated to Washington, D.C., from Russia, where Jolson was born Asa Yoelson, the son of a cantor, in 1886. The youngster ran away from home twice to join the circus. He made his stage debut in "The Children of the Ghetto" at the Herald Square Theatre in New York City, after which he joined the famous Lew Dockstader minstrel show. It was while with this organization that Al donned blackface for the first time, a feature that would quickly become his trademark. With the Dockstader show, Al sharpened his song and dance talents.

Al Jolson, in person.

To many, Jolson appeared to be his own biggest fan, but those who knew the man also realized that the only thing bigger than Jolson's gigantic ego was his talent.

Now we jump ahead almost seven decades, and guess what? Al Jolson has returned to entertain his fans once again. But I tell a lie. It isn't really Al Jolson (he died suddenly in 1950), but rather British entertainer Brian Conley, who many say is more like Jolson than Jolson himself. Jolson, er, Conley, stars in *Jolson, the Musical,* which premiers tomorrow at Toronto's beautiful Royal Alexandra Theatre and runs until August 2, 1997.

It's only fitting that the North American premier of this show, which comes to us from London's Victoria Palace theatre, should be here in Toronto, since Al spent so much time in our city. In fact, I can remember reading somewhere that as a young man Jolson worked as a bellhop in one of Toronto's seedy downtown hotels. And while I can't remember where I read the article, the young man must have been here in the very early years of this century since by the time he was 25 Al had been discovered and was working for the Shubert brothers in New York City.

I also recall that the story described Jolson's less than flattering opinion of our city, saying that he couldn't wait to get out of town since there wasn't much for a young man to do in Toronto the good.

Well, as much as Al Jolson may have disliked Toronto at first, the world of show business soon gave him a change of heart, and before long he had become a frequent visitor. Thanks to research done by Robert Brockhouse at Mirvish Productions we do know that Al's first stage appearance in our city was at the Royal Alexandra, though the choice of that theatre wasn't Jolson's. In fact, the Alex was the Toronto venue for all Shubert productions.

Al came to town in early January, 1913, and appeared on the Alex's stage with a very young comedienne named Fanny Brice in a musical titled *The Whirl of Society*. Actually the prime billing for that vaudeville performance went to Gaby Deslys, who was described as a "vivacious French dancer whose name alone is enough to bring out the audiences." There's no record of how Jolson reacted to being upstaged in this way, although we can assume he wasn't particularly happy with the second billing.

Jolson returned in mid-December of the same year to star in *Honeymoon Express* and again in 1915 as the lead in *Dancing Around*. The next year he appeared in *Robinson Crusoe, Jr.*, in 1920 in *Sinbad*, and in 1923 in *Bombo*. Four years later, in 1927, he was back in *Big Boy* . He returned in 1941 for one last stage appearance in *Hold on to Your Hats*. By this time Jolson knew Toronto well enough to get a laugh from his audience by calling Dufferin Park, a long-time city horse-racing track that stood where the Dufferin Mall is today, "Sufferin' Park." Each time Al played Toronto it was on the friendly stage of the Royal Alexandra Theatre.

Interestingly, *The Whirl of Society*, *Robinson Crusoe, Jr.*, *Sinbad*, *Bombo*, and *Big Boy* were all seen by Toronto audiences long before these musicals opened on Broadway.

And while it's true that Jolson was first seen here in musicals, most Torontonians would remember him best as the star of a film that would become a pivotal point in the history of motion pictures, *The Jazz Singer*. It was first screened in October of 1927, and New York City audiences were stunned when they heard Jolson, the star of the film, talk and sing. This was achieved by playing a recorded disc that was synchronized with Jolson's mouthing of the words. Historians agree that this was the first successful feature-length talking movie. But by the time it got to the silver screen of the Tivoli Theatre here in Toronto on January 18, 1929, the movie was old hat. In fact, it displaced an all-talking feature titled *The Terror*.

Al Jolson, star of stage, screen, radio and phonograph recordings died on October 23, 1950, while playing cards.

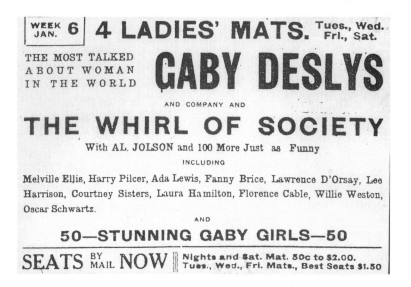

Al Jolson's name is barely visible in this ad for his first Toronto appearance at the Royal Alexandra Theatre, January 6 to 11, 1913.

NEW BELLS ARE READY TO PEAL
AT ST. JAMES'

June 22, 1997

This year marks the 200th anniversary of the founding of what we know as St. James' Cathedral, Toronto's very first church. In its first few years it was known simply as the church at York, York being our community's name before it was elevated to the City of Toronto in 1834. In fact, it wasn't until 1828 that this pioneer house of worship finally got a name following its dedication to St. James the Apostle by the Bishop of the day, the Rt. Rev. Charles James Stewart. I'm assured that although the good bishop's middle name was James,

This striking turn-of-the-century penny postcard of St. James' shows the 1853 cathedral with its tower (completed in 1865) and 324-foot-high spire (completed in 1874). The sound of the new peal of bells emanates from the louvred openings, just below the clock, which can be closed during practice sessions.

that fact had no influence on his selection of the church's name.

And here's a little Toronto street trivia. The church's location, originally on the Town of York's western outskirts, was precisely why the nearby thoroughfare was given the name Church Street, as the dusty (or muddy, depending on the weather) path through the woods led to the city's pioneer house of worship.

One of the most recognizable features of the present-day cathedral (a title bestowed on the church in 1840) is the sound of its

During the week of March 3 to 7, 1997, workmen carefully installed the new old bells in the church's tower through openings incorporated in the old church structure, perhaps confirming the belief that a full peal of bells was anticipated for the church when it was erected 144 years ago. (photo courtesy Connie Robson)

bells, nine of which were installed in the tower in 1865, with a tenth added in 1928. This peal of ten bells does not ring forth tunes, but rather what's referred to as traditional English changes announcing the quarter hours. A separate keyboard also permits change-ringing patterns in carillon fashion.

In anticipation of the cathedral's upcoming bicentennial, a group calling itself the Bells of Old York was established several years ago and adopted as its goal the acquisition and installation of a full peal of 12 "English Change-Ringing Bells" high in the church tower. Incidentally, the technique of change ringing, recognized by many as both folk art and science, was developed in England during the Renaissance. Its introduction at the Cathedral Church of St. James' will be a first in our province.

Funds for this inspired project, as well as the money necessary to modify and upgrade the tower to accommodate more than six tons of new bells and ancillary equipment, was raised entirely from public subscription; no church funds were involved. By the way, the ten original bells will remain in place in the tower.

Now, while I've been referring to the addition to the tower as a peal of new bells, in fact, only two of the dozen are truly new, the two having been cast at the Whitechapel Foundry, London, just last year. Ten others are bells that have, since 1828, peeled forth from the tower of another church dedicated to St. James, this time St. James' Church, Bermondsey, South London, England. Two of these 1828 bells were recast in 1996, with the other eight being true originals. This peal will be the first of this magnitude on the continent. There are peals of ten bells in three other North American cities, one of which is Victoria, B.C.

Unlike St. James' Cathedral's original ten bells (the ones that strike the quarter hours), which are fixed in position and ring out when hammers strike the outside lip of the bell, the new peal of 12 bells are rung by specially trained bell ringers who, by pulling on ropes connected to wheels, cause the bells (the lightest weighs in at 630 pounds, the heaviest at 2 400 pounds) to rotate on a fixed axis. A distinctive sound, unique to each bell, occurs when the bell's free-swinging clapper strikes the inside of the bell at a predetermined spot as the bell rotates. The term *change ringing* describes the activity performed by the bell ringers that results in the bells changing in sequence each time they ring out. A change-ringing program can be several hours in length.

As important as the new peal of bells will be, it would all be for naught without the dedicated group (throng, party, chime?) of more than 30 volunteer bell ringers, who have been training for the past several months.

The project will culminate this coming Friday when, at 5:00 p.m., Toronto's newest voice will ring out proclaiming the success of the Bells of Old York project. The public is invited to gather on the lawn around the cathedral, and in the park adjacent. Why not bring folding chairs and a picnic dinner and enjoy this inaugural concert?

A short concert featuring St. James' new peal of bells can be heard each Sunday morning at 10:15.

SUNNYSIDE'S 75TH ANNIVERSARY

June 28, 1997

It was exactly 75 years ago today that Torontonians were told to go jump in the lake. And guess what? They did, and by the thousands. The suggestion was made by Mayor Alf McGuire, who had just declared the city's new Sunnyside Bathing Pavilion and the nearby amusement park officially open.

That's not to say that citizens hadn't taken advantage of the cool (often cold) lake waters off Sunnyside Beach in the past. In fact, old photographs show bathers enjoying outings down at Sunnyside as far back as the 1880s.

During the park's inaugural year, thousands took advantage of the facilities provided in the new bathing pavilion to change into swimsuits followed by hours of lolling about on the new and improved beach (sand for which had been brought in specially from a farm in Pickering, Ontario) and a leisurely dip in the lake. Unfortunately, the summers of 1923 and 1924 were anything but warm, so swimmers stayed out of the lake (and away from Sunnyside's games, rides, and hot dog stands) in droves. In hopes of alleviating the problem, officials of the Toronto Harbour Commission, who had built the pavilion and park as part of its mutlimillion-dollar plan to develop the waterfront from the Humber as far east as Victoria Park, decided to build a swimming facility that would feature heated and filtered water and would be large enough to accommodate as many as 2 000 swimmers a day. In an effort to justify the tank's $75 000 price tag, officials gave it the grandiose title Sunnyside Outdoor Natatorium. Locals, however, never did take to the fancy name. For them it was simply the tank, and those who insisted on calling it the pool were obviously from some other planet.

With the opening of the new bathing pavilion and amusement park on June 28, 1922, it wasn't long before thousands got into the habit of visiting the city's newest summertime attraction. They got there on foot, by car, and more often than not, by streetcar. For children, there was the special free bathing car that would wander city streets Once there they would spend the day on the rides, playing games of skill and chance, and gorging themselves at the numerous food stands and restaurants.

They also came to Sunnyside for the dances that were held in the former Walter Dean boat factory, which in the winter of 1921 had been transformed into a magical place called the Palais Royale.

For the next 33 years the amusement park, albeit showing its age as the end approached, was a major attraction in a much less sophisticated Toronto. And while the rides and snack bars closed forever in the fall of 1955, the bathing pavilion and Palais Royale still attract thousands each year to Sunnyside Beach.

Sunnyside Amusement Park, 1929.

To learn more about Sunnyside read Mike Filey's I Remember Sunnyside *(Dundurn Press).*

DEDICATED TO ANARCHY

June 29, 1997

Emma Goldman (1869–1940)

Once again, Toronto theatre audiences have a treasure trove of excellent plays and musicals to choose from, and with *Show Boat* returning later this year that selection only gets better. In my opinion, one of the best now playing is *Ragtime*, now on stage at the Ford Centre for the Performing Arts in North York. Another Drabinsky triumph, *Ragtime* is a theatricalization of E. L. Doctorow's acclaimed 1975 novel of the same name. Like the book, the play focuses on the turbulent years between the start of this century and the outbreak of the Great War. The main characters of the work are fictional and represent turn-of-the-century American families from three distinct social strata — upper-middle-class white Anglo-Saxon Protestant, socialist immigrant Jewish, and Harlem black — each family with its own hopes and dreams, each plagued by the disparities and inequalities between the classes. I was particularly intrigued by the historical characters who parade through the musical. Luminaries such as industrialist Henry Ford, educator Booker T. Washington, the crime-of-the-century trio consisting of architect Stanford White, chorus girl Evelyn Nesbit, and her husband, Harry K. Thaw, explorer Admiral Robert Peary, and anarchist Emma Goldman help position *Ragtime* in history's almanac.

Amongst this list of celebrities, students of Toronto's past will find Emma Goldman of special interest. Born in Lithuania in 1869, Emma moved to St. Petersburg, Russia, with her family when the youngster was 12. Four years later the family emigrated to the United States, settling in Rochester, New York, where Emma obtained work in a garment factory sewing ulsters (long cloth overcoats), spending 10 hours every day at her sewing machine. For this she received a weekly pay check of $2.50!

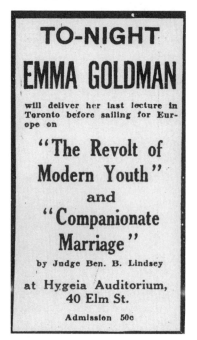

Ad for Emma's controversial lecture held in Hygeia Hall, 40 Elm Street, on February 7, 1928.

This harsh treatment of newly arrived immigrants was but one of the factors that led to Emma's quest to seek equality amongst the races as well as between the sexes. In the simplest terms, Emma envisioned "a communist society of free individuals linked through a federated association, contributing according to ability and taking according to need."

Unfortunately, her perceived complicity in the violent 1892 Homestead steel plant riot (in which ten workers and three Pinkerton security police were killed) as well as her remote association with the man who assassinated William McKinley during the president's September, 1901, visit to the Pan-American Exposition in Buffalo resulted in Emma being branded an anarchist. Unable to prove its case, the government continued to persecute her, and when Red Emma, as she became known, began to publicly promote the idea of birth control, that was too much. For this indiscretion, she was jailed. With the outbreak of war in Europe in 1914, it wasn't long before war hysteria began sweeping the United States. When she again spoke out, this time against the draft, Emma was again jailed and eventually deported to Russia along with other nonconforming dissidents, in spite of the fact she was an American citizen as a result of her marriage to an American soon after her arrival in the States.

Finding even less freedom in Russia than in the States, Emma was on the move again. This time she obtained British citizenship through an arranged marriage and then embarked on a speaking tour that never included visits to the States, but often attracted interested Americans to her appearances in Toronto and Montreal. At her February 7, 1928, talk at Toronto's Hygeia Hall, 40 Elm Street, Emma spoke out in favour of companionate marriage, birth control, and easy divorce, all red-hot topics of the day. A collection amounting to nearly $100 was raised and in typical Emma Goldman fashion was sent to the striking miners in Ohio and Pennsylvania. During her several stays in our city she lived in a third-floor flat over Sammy Kruger's restaurant at 322 Spadina Avenue. In April 1940, following a visit to Spain, where she had spoken out in support of the anarchists being pummelled in that country's violent civil war, she retired to her small flat in Toronto. It was in our city that on May 14, 1940, Emma Goldman died. Her remains were interred in a Chicago, Illinois, cemetery.

Emma's Toronto home consisted of a couple of small rooms on the third floor at 322 Spadina Avenue, the building at the left of this trio located on the west side of Spadina, just north of Dundas.

YES, SIR HENRY'S HOME REALLY WAS HIS CASTLE

July 6, 1997

Sir Henry Pellatt (with walking stick) was guest of honour at a luncheon held at the castle on August 12, 1938. With him are U.S. Consul General H.C. Hengstler (left) and William Bothwell (right), president of the Kiwanis Club of West Toronto and the man whose suggestion that the service club operate Casa Loma as a tourist attraction breathed new life into the troubled castle.

A couple of years ago I was asked to accompany a group of women from the States as they toured the city with a stopover at Casa Loma. The dream of industrialist and financier Sir Henry Pellatt, the castle (which some describe as a combination of Scottish battlement and French chateau architecture, though others suggest its appearance is more 20th Century Fox than anything) was built by Sir Henry in the early teens at a cost of $1.7 million. By the way, those are 1913 dollars. Today the castle is estimated to be worth more than $36 million, with the nearby stables adding another $5.4 million.

Of course, the most frequent question asked by visitors to Casa Loma is why in the world anyone would build the thing in the first place. To fully understand the answer one would have to know Sir Henry. In addition to his other traits, he was perhaps the world's greatest monarchist, and was concerned that should his beloved king and queen decide to visit Toronto, they must have a proper place in which to stay. No high-class hotels or pseudo mansions for them. They'd stay in a castle, his castle, Casa Loma.

Unfortunately for Sir Henry, royalty never had the opportunity to stay at the Pellatt residence. In fact, even the Pellatt family's stay wasn't all that long. Dinged by a couple of financial setbacks followed by the city's determination to have the castle undergo something called market-value reassessment — as a result of which the property tax bill skyrocketed from $50,000 in 1912 to $250,000 in 1913 — Sir Henry reluctantly abandoned his abode, a place some had laughingly dubbed "Chateau Pellatt."

As the result of non-payment of property taxes, ownership of the castle reverted to the city. Subsequently, a number of possible uses for place were explored. Some thought it could be the home of a relocated Hospital for Sick Children (at the time the hospital was on College Street at Elizabeth). Mary Pickford suggested it might become her Canadian residence. Someone proposed the castle as a great location for wax museum. And the CPR considered it, briefly, as a grand railway station feeding passengers to its nearby rail line. Toronto architect William Sparling even tried operating the castle as a hotel, complete with a musical group for the visitors' dining and dancing pleasure. Unfortunately, that project also failed, and again the castle's massive doors swung shut. (Incidentally, the musical group eventually became famous as Glen Gray and the Casa Loma Orchestra.) With no real answer to the problem, in 1934 city politician George Ramsden was trying to talk council into requesting a demolition permit to level the building. That would certainly end the problem.

Fortunately, wiser heads prevailed and the permit was never issued. Instead, the Kiwanis Club of West Toronto requested that it be given the authority to operate the castle as a tourist attraction. The club's proposition was approved and on July 10, 1937, Casa Loma opened to the public on the understanding that a portion of the income from admission and rental fees be turned over to the city. The remainder was earmarked for various charitable purposes. In addition, the club would pay those ever-present property taxes.

Sixty years later, Kiwanis continues to operate Casa Loma on a financially self-sufficient basis without government grants or subsidies. In fact, between 1992 and 1996, the club paid the city nearly $274,000 in property taxes, turned over another $3.3 million to the city in licensing fees, and donated a further $1.5 million to various charities.

Major League Baseball's traditional All-Star Game will be held this coming Tuesday in Cleveland. This year special tribute is being paid to Jackie Robinson who in 1947 (and in the words of the Associate Press report filed April 10 of that year) "became the first of his race to break into modern major league baseball when the Brooklyn Dodgers purchased his contract from the Montreal Royals of the International League."

Interestingly, Jackie was seen by Torontonians for the first time during a game played on May 17, 1946, at the old Maple Leaf Stadium, which occupied the southwest corner of Lake Shore Boulevard West and Bathurst Street from 1926 until 1968. The game was won by Montreal 5 to 4. *Telegram* newspaper icon Ted Reeve, writing the following day about the Royals' big second baseman, suggested that the youngster's chances of reaching the big leagues weren't very good. Not because of Robinson's colour, but because of a certain stiffness in his shoulders resulting from injuries received during his football playing days in the States.

Jackie Robinson was guest of honour at the Variety Club's "Baseball Night" at Maple Leaf Stadium in 1962. In the photo Jackie, wearing a Leaf uniform, signs autographs for several young guests of the Variety Club.

REMEMBERING SUNNY DAYS GONE BY

July 20, 1997

In a recent column I asked readers to submit their best photographs that show our city and its environs in the good old summertime of yesteryear. Here are a couple of examples of the good old summertime photos I'm looking for.

Mom and the kids get ready to board one of the big radial streetcars for a ride into cottage country, summer, 1910.

In the first photo, taken in the summer of 1910, someone has snapped mom and the kids waiting to board the big green streetcar of the Toronto and York Radial Railway at the line's southern terminal on Yonge Street opposite the site of the former North Toronto railway station. Maybe they're on their way to cottage country to visit the kids' grandparents near Filey Beach (there really is such a place on the south shore of Lake Simcoe), or perhaps they're off to see an aunt and uncle in Newmarket or Aurora. The large streetcar they are about to board was called a radial car, a name adopted because these cars operated over track that radiated out from Toronto to places like Guelph,

Georgetown, Woodbridge, and, in this case, Sutton and Jackson's Point. A number of other radial lines were proposed, but the popularity of the automobile eventually brought the radials to the end of their tracks.

Nevertheless riding the radials was a favourite way of getting out of town in the summers of yesteryear.

Incidentally, this photo was easy to date thanks to the poster attached to the wall of the station. It advertises another summer attraction the good old Exhibition, a popular event that continues to this day. Got any old day at the Ex pictures?

In the second photo, date unknown, someone has taken a photograph of this handsome couple driving through what is still a favourite summer playground for thousands to this very day. In fact, picturesque High Park has become so popular on summer weekends it's now closed to vehicular traffic.

Mom and dad out for a summertime spin through High Park in the old man's new Northern automobile.

This form of transportation would have been a real eye-grabber back in the early days of the century, since what was referred to as a horseless carriage was still very much a novelty around town. While we're not sure when the photo was taken I have been told the car in the photo is a Northern, a pioneer gasoline-engine vehicle introduced in 1902.

TRACK TO THE FUTURE

July 27, 1997

At one time Belt Line streetcars operated on Spadina Avenue.

At 1:00 p.m. this afternoon, Metro Toronto will see the length of its streetcar routes increased by exactly 2.27 miles (3.65 km.) with the official opening of the brand new 510 Spadina line.

This addition is of particular significance when one recalls that years ago those in the know had set the year 1980 as the date when all streetcar operations in Toronto would end forever.

Historically speaking (or writing), the new Spadina line, which will operate over a reserved right-of-way down the centre of Spadina Avenue from the Bloor-Danforth subway to Queen's Quay, revives, to a certain degree, one of Toronto's earliest streetcar lines, one that was opened by the privately owned Toronto Street Railway Company 118 years ago. With that opening, many citizens living in the Spadina and College neighborhood could use the horse-drawn cars that traversed the newly laid tracks on Spadina Avenue and connect with the existing King Street trackage to get to and from the busy St. Lawrence Market.

In 1891, the street became the west leg of the new belt line route, which utilized tracks on Bloor, Sherbourne, King, and Spadina to form a belt around downtown Toronto. One year later, the horse-drawn cars were replaced by electric cars.

Passengers wait to board the Spadina double-ended streetcar at the Bloor Street corner some time during the war

The Spadina streetcar at the south end of the line in the 1930s.

Two years after the TTC took over all city streetcar operations in 1921, the unique belt line route ended following the Commission's reintroduction of another Spadina streetcar line. This one traversed the broad thoroughfare from Bloor to Front, with a southerly extension over the railway tracks to Queen's Quay. It opened in 1927. The cars used on this line were double-ended, eliminating the need for loops.

On October 10, 1948, all Spadina streetcars were removed to be replaced by buses in an attempt to conserve electricity, in short supply following the end of the Second World War.

Now, nearly 50 years after the last Spadina car trundled along the avenue, streetcars are once again back on Spadina. Official opening ceremonies will take place on a stage just south of Spadina and Bloor.

MACKENZIE'S MANSIONS

August 3, 1997

I know it's not nice to refer to our historical icons as having heads made out of wood, but that's exactly what's happened to Sir William Mackenzie, referred to in his day as Canada's Railway King. Sir William was born in Kirkfield, Ontario, a pretty little community on the modern-day Highway 48 between Beaverton and Coboconk in 1849. His early successes in the lumber business allowed him to build a substantial residence in his hometown into which he and his wife moved in 1888.

Statue unveiling at the Sir William Mackenzie Inn, July 21, 1997.

Mackenzie's subsequent business activities included the establishment of the Toronto Railway Company, forerunner of the TTC, and the Electric Development Corporation (to generate and transmit power from the Falls to Toronto) as well as the creation of Brazilian Traction, an enterprise that has evolved into the huge Brascan empire, and, with friend and business partner Sir Donald Mann, the construction of the Canadian Northern Railway. By 1915 its tracks connected Halifax on the east coast with Victoria on the west. In 1911, Mackenzie was knighted for his outstanding business achievements, which enhanced both Canada and the British Empire.

In an effort to get closer to the action, in 1897 Mackenzie purchased S. H. Janes' Benvenuto, a palatial mansion on the Avenue Road hill, which the developer of what is know known as the Annex had commissioned six years earlier. Mackenzie kept his Kirkfield residence as a summer retreat. He died at Benvenuto on December 5, 1923. As he had requested, his burial in the little Kirkfield cemetery was conducted without the pomp and circumstance befitting a man of Sir William's stature.

Inn owner Paul Scott introduces the creators of the Sir William sculpture, Donna Pascoe and Peter Turrell, July 21, 1997.

Benvenuto, built in 1892 on the Avenue Road hill south of St. Clair Avenue, as it looked when Sir William was in residence. Only its massive stone wall remains today.

So how do I get off referring to Sir William as a wooden head? Let me explain. On July 15, 1995, a terrific windstorm ravaged Kirkfield, and in the process toppled more than 100 large trees that had been planted by Lady Mackenzie on the grounds surrounding the Mackenzie house more than a century earlier. The distraught owners of the house, Joan and Paul Scott, who had only recently converted the former mansion into a charming bed and breakfast, called the Sir William

Mackenzie Inn, decided to turn Mother Nature's devastation into a sculpture garden by commissioning a number of wood carvers to use their talents to convert some of the mangled trees into stately wooden monuments. One year later their work was done. But there was one tree left, a special one, standing, as it did, albeit forlornly, right in front of the house. Grand Valley, Ontario, artists Peter Turrell and Donna Pascoe were given the honour of giving the tree new life, and on the afternoon of July 21, 1997, Sir William Mackenzie came home when his life-size likeness, fashioned from the trunk of the devastated pine tree, was unveiled.

Sir William Mackenzie in wood.

Sir William Mackenzie. His fascinating story is told in *The Railway King* by Rae Fleming (UBC Press, 1991).

TAKING A MILK RUN ALONG SPADINA

August 10, 1997

The recent opening of the Spadina streetcar line (some insist it be called an LRT — Light Rail Transit — line, but we all know it's really an upgraded streetcar line) has done wonders for one of the city's most interesting thoroughfares. Top of the list, of course, is the fact that today's Spadina transit patrons have a ride much improved over the trip experienced on the buses that wandered in and out of traffic as they lurched their way, often in packs, from stop to stop. And streetcars don't belch sickly diesel fumes, either. Now if we could get the car and truck drivers to heed the new traffic alignment pattern and traffic signals.... Incidentally, for those who may not be aware, those white diamond shapes painted on the streetcar right-of-way mean *keep off*. And the term *transit signal* really means *this is the signal the streetcars obey*. It's amazing to stand at an intersection and watch how many car driver's think it's their signal. Bam!

Turn-of-the-century postcard view of the City Dairy on Spadina Crescent.

Adding to the improved appearance of Spadina is a collection of public art pieces commissioned by the TTC in an effort to "express the character of Spadina Avenue by celebrating its rich history and cultural heritage," to quote from the press release. The funding for the eight commissions came from the Province of Ontario and the

Municipality of Metropolitan Toronto, the latter being involved since Spadina Avenue is designated as a Metro road, a definition that will disappear with the birth of the megacity at the end of the year.

Same view, July 28, 1997. The old Belt Line streetcar was replaced by the new 510 Spadina streetcar, which began service on July 28, 1997.

As with most artistic creations, the story behind these creations, while in many cases interesting, usually remains with the artist while the public ponders over what it all means. Perhaps one day a pamphlet profiling the stories behind the Spadina artwork will be available in the restaurants and shops along the street and even on the Spadina streetcars.

While I like the cat on the chair, the silhouetted streetcar, and the Chinese dragon, one of the pieces that's of particular interest to me and, I'll bet, to those who can remember those far off days when the milkman and his horse-drawn wagon were frequent visitors is the giant City Dairy milk bottle at the corner of Spadina and Willcocks.

Its location high atop a 20-foot pole in the centre boulevard is not far from the former City Dairy factory that still stands on Spadina Crescent directly east of the landmark Knox College in Spadina Circle.

City Dairy was established by several civic-minded businessman to provide citizens with a source of milk prepared using the most scientific and sanitary conditions then available. This was in stark contrast to existing methods whereby milk from cows kept in sheds behind houses in various parts of the city was transported to retailers in open containers and to the customer by simply transferring it into whatever was handy using less-than-hygienic dippers and ladles. The City Dairy factory and office complex on Spadina Crescent opened in 1900 and for years was a favourite stop for courting couples who, travelling on the belt line streetcars that glided by the front door (streetcars once again glide by the old building), would purchase nickel ice cream cones and milk shakes. City Dairy was acquired by Borden's in 1930, though the City Dairy name wasn't phased out for another nine years. Borden's remained at the Spadina Crescent address until the fall of 1963. Both the former dairy and nearby Knox College are now occupied by departments of the University of Toronto.

Artist Stephen Cruise's milk bottle, complete with the original City Dairy logo, overlooks the Spadina and Willcocks intersection, 1997.

I REMEMBER A VERY SPECIAL EX

August 17, 1997

Ever since 1879, when a group of far-sighted city fathers and businessmen presented the premier edition of their collective creation, citizens and visitors to our fair city alike have flocked to what's become known, with affection, as the grand old lady of the waterfront, or simply the Ex.

Like most Torontonians, my first visit to the fair was not of my own choosing. Since my parents were Ex goers, when that special time of year rolled around, like it or not, I too became a visitor, albeit one more interested in the kiddie rides than in the furniture items featured at the Eaton display in the mammoth Manufacturers' Building. Now, while I don't remember exactly when my first solo trip to the fair took place, I do recall wandering through the buildings eagerly gathering up covers for my schoolbooks and as many small wooden rulers (marked off in inches, not whatever it is they use today) as I could in dreaded anticipation of soon returning to the hallowed halls of John Fisher Public School.

While all visits to the Ex were special, one year sticks in my mind as being extra special. In 1956 I was 15, an experienced high school student about to embark on my second year at North Toronto Collegiate. I had developed a fascination for airplanes, and what made the 1956 Ex so special was that was the year the Air Show was first held during the fair. Previously it had been a totally separate event, held initially at Dufferin (now Downsview) Airport, then down on the waterfront south of the Exhibition Grounds, but at a time other than Exhibition time.

Now, for any airplane nut the list of participating aircraft at that first CNE International Air Show today reads like the roster of the world's best aviation museum. There were Vampires, Sabres, CF-100s, Mustangs (long before Ford usurped the name), C-119s (nicknamed "Packets" or "Flying Boxcars"), Cougars flown by the Blue Angels, an ultra-modern B-47 (its H-bombs left at home on orders from Ottawa), and a KC-97 in-flight refueller, a mammoth 10-engine B-36 (the newspaper said it was too large to land in Canada and flew here from its base in the States — wow!), the Navy's Neptune patrol craft,

Lumberjack Paul Bunyan gazes down on visitors to the Ontario Government Building.

and its new Banshee jets, Beavers, Otters, a North Star (the TCA pilot even spoke to the crowd) — this was heaven.

Something else sticks in my mind from the 1956 fair. In the open courtyard of the Ontario Government Building (now the CNE Casino), towering over the cages of wildlife and fish borrowed from provincial forests, was an enormous, 24-foot-high seated likeness of mythical folklore hero Paul Bunyan garbed in a green and black checked lumberjack shirt, pants, and a huge pair of boots. I seem to recall that his mighty blue ox, Babe, was there, too, but of this I'm not completely sure. By the way, for younger readers Paul Bunyan created the Great Lakes and the Rocky Mountains. Or so they say.

And in the nearby Governments Building (now Medieval Times), the United Kingdom featured a scale model of Calder Hall, the world's first large-scale nuclear power station, which the Queen would officially open on October 17, 1956, a couple of Rolls-Royce and Bristol cut-away jet engines, and a real colour television camera and receiving set. In the same building, Japan, described as the "New" Japan, displayed cameras and furniture. In the always popular Food Building visitors could watch what "the northern Eskimo" cooks in an igloo kitchen. Gettin' hungry? Just outside was the big Shopsy booth. What's a visit to the Ex with out a Shopsy hot dog?

The afternoon Grandstand Show featured "the singing (but no smooching) cowboy" Gene Autry and his screen leading lady, Annie Oakley, a.k.a. Gail Davis. Gene and Annie flew into Toronto in Gene's private plane, and Gene's horse, Champion, arrived via special railway car. For the adults, the evening Grandstand Show featured the Canadettes and the RCMP Musical Ride. In 1956 they tried a cross-lake swim marathon that, due to the cold water, nobody completed. Nevertheless, Port Credit's Elizabeth Schopf managed to water-ski from Niagara-on-the-Lake to the CNE in two hours. Gene, Annie, and Champion I remember. Elizabeth I don't. For kids young and old, the Ex was and still is an amazing place!

And what's a trip to the Ex without a Shopsy's corned beef sandwich? You bought them at this special booth that was located just outside the Food Building.

CNE'S HERITAGE IS ON DISPLAY

August 24, 1997

Visitors to this year's Ex have the opportunity, while strolling the grounds, to visit both the very old and the very new, the very old being Toronto's oldest house, Scadding Cabin (west of the band shell and staffed by knowledgeable members of the York Pioneers) and the very new, the striking National Trade Centre just inside the Princes' Gates.

The Electrical and Engineering Building, erected in 1928, demolished in 1972, now the site of the National Trade Centre. Close-up of one of the original Statues of Industry (see arrow) now on view in Heritage Court.

Pioneer settler John Scadding built his cabin on the banks of the Don River near today's Queen Street in 1794. Coincident with the opening of the first Exhibition in 1879, the tiny cabin was disassembled, moved, and reassembled on its present site.

The National Trade Centre, an eagerly anticipated addition to the grounds for decades, was officially opened earlier this year. While the building may be bright and shiny and new, the people charged with creating the new trade centre cleverly incorporated traces of earlier exhibition structures within its massive shell. Externally, the building's east facade mimics the 1929 Automotive Building across Princes' Boulevard. And in the evening searchlights return to the Ex in the form of powerful beams emanating from the centre's massive quartet of towers.

One of the original "Statues of Industry" now preserved in the National Trade Centre's Heritage Court.

During a visit to the Garden Show in Heritage Court (located right where the old east entrance streetcar loop use to be), visitors can view the beautifully restored south facade of the 1922 Royal Coliseum, a structure that in its time was as spectacular as the new trade centre is today. Standing guard in front of the Coliseum are four of the eight towering Statues of Industry, which originally gazed out upon Exhibition crowds from their perch atop the Electrical and Engineering Building. This imposing structure was erected in 1928 as part of an ancient master plan for the grounds. From that year until the building's demolition 25 years ago for the "imminent" construction of a trade centre building (the site remained a parking lot for almost the entire time, though someone had the foresight to preserve the statues for future reuse), the Electrical and Engineering Building was the place to discover the very latest in inventions. From radios to refrigerators, stoves to stereos, you name it, if it was new, the Ex, recognized as "the Showplace of the Nation," would have it first.

Interestingly, this year's Festival of the Future feature, located in Salon D in the Trade Centre Building, brings that very concept back to the Ex.

By the way, while you're in Salon D be sure to see the CNE Archives exhibit, "Progress on Display, Science and Technology at the CNE Since 1879." It'll sure bring back memories.

In the corridor next to Salon D another part of the CNE's heritage has been retained. Many CNE visitors will remember the eight huge murals depicting the early history of exploration and trading that could be seen encircling the interior of the dome of the former Arts, Crafts and Hobbies Building (first called the

Artist Fred Haines (1878–1960)

One of the eight Fred Haines murals painted in 1929 and now on view in the National Trade Centre.

Governments Building, and now Medieval Times) at the west end of the grounds. These paintings were done by Fred Haines and some of his students at the Ontario College of Art back in 1929. Removed from the old building in 1993 and placed in storage, these wonderful pieces of Canadiana have been lovingly restored by Hamilton based conservator Elizabeth Shambrook and now grace the walls at the east end of the National Trade Centre.

Back in Heritage Court, other sculptures and architectural elements from the CNE's past have been preserved in the form of livestock medallions, keystones, and tympanum and cornice pieces from the various buildings comprising the Coliseum complex.

While the CNE is frequently criticized for the way it treats its past, in my opinion this time they "done good." Among the key players that made it all work are Metro Councillor Joe Pantalone, NTC Project Director Roger Floyd, art consultant Karen Mills, CNE Works Manager Gord Walker, and Edwin Rouse of ERA Architect Inc.

REMEMBERING THE OTHER PRINCE

August 31, 1997

A true Toronto landmark, the Princes' Gates, 1997.

As this year's edition of the good old Canadian National Exhibition winds down, thousands of fair goers will enter and leave the grounds through the massive Princes' Gates.

Erected exactly 70 years ago as just one component of the massive redevelopment plan for the east end of the grounds, a plan that would see the construction of the Electrical and Engineering Building in 1928 and the Automotive Building the following year, the entranceway was scheduled to be known as the Diamond Jubilee of Confederation Gate. It would commemorate the sixty years that had passed since the confederation of Canada's original four provinces in 1867.

Fortunately (at least for those who were easily tongue-tied) two members of the Commonwealth's Royal family were scheduled to visit Toronto in the summer of 1927, and as part of their busy schedule they would be asked to officially open two of the bustling city's new landmarks-to-be. The first, Toronto's new Union Station, had actually been completed seven years earlier except for the alignment of tracks, a rather important feature of any railway station. It wasn't until Edward, the Prince of Wales, accompanied by his younger brother Prince George, unlocked the impressive station's main door on August 8, 1927, that it looked as if the station would finally be open for business. Actually, another three days would go by before the public was allowed in.

The boys then agreed to return later in the month, following their brief visit to the future king's ranch in Alberta, to officially dedicate another of the bustling city's monumental new structures. This time it would be the Exhibition's just completed eastern entrance, the one with the rather wordy name. This they did 70 years ago yesterday, August 30, 1927. The term Diamond Jubilee of Confederation Gate was dropped almost immediately, and the now familiar Princes' Gates adopted.

Several weeks before the Gates were dedicated the princes arrived at the old Union Station to officially open the new Union Station. The Prince of Wales (right) chats with Lieutenant Governor Ross while Prince George (in the naval uniform) walks a few steps behind him, August 26, 1927.

In truth, describing the name as "familiar" may not be correct, since many continue to call it the Princess Gates as if the structure had been named in honour of a female member of the Royal family. Please! Princes', male, plural.

Today, almost everyone knows what befell the Prince of Wales, a man described by some historians as the king we lost. Following the death of his father, King George V, on January 20, 1936, Edward assumed the throne as King Edward VIII, only to abdicate on December 10, 1936, so that he could marry American divorcee Wallace Simpson. Edward was succeeded by Prince Albert, who became King George VI. Still with me?

But what about the other prince in the Princes' Gates title, the one that makes the word plural?

Edward, Prince of Wales cuts a ribbon to officially open the new Princes' Gates. Behind him, wearing the light grey suit, is the other prince, Prince George. August 30, 1927.

H.R.H. Prince George Edward Alexander Edmund Windsor, Duke of Kent, Earl of St. Andrew (and a number of other titles) was the youngest son of the late King George V and the youngest of four princes each one highly respected by the people of Canada. Prince George had a special affiliation with the citizens of Toronto having visited our city twice in 1927 and again in 1941, at which time he officially opened that year's CNE, the last to be held before the fairgrounds were put off limits for the duration of the war.

With the outbreak of war in the fall of 1939 Prince George assumed the title of Air Commodore. He was also assigned the role of Senior Welfare Officer, and it was while performing in this capacity that the prince decided to pay a visit to the Royal Air Force stations in Iceland.

Early in the afternoon on Tuesday, August 25, 1942, the 39-year-old prince boarded one of the RAF's cumbersome Sunderland flying boats, W-4026 "M" of 228 Squadron, that sat bobbing up and down in the harbour in Invergordon, a community nestled on the shore of Cromarty Firth on the northeast coast of Scotland. It was assumed that the 900-mile flight would take the lumbering aircraft approximately seven hours to execute. Sadly, not only did the plane with the prince and 14 other individuals on board not complete its trip, the aircraft never made it out of Scotland. Exactly 42 minutes after it lifted from the water, W-4026 slammed into a barren Scottish hillside below a place called Eagle's Rock. All but the rear turret air gunner, Flight Sergeant Andrew Jack, who, on impact, was thrown clear of the flaming wreckage, died in the tragedy.

To this day, researchers cannot agree on the reason for the crash and the popular Duke's untimely death. Some suggested it was an act of sabotage while others blamed the pilot for not seeking a higher altitude when the visibility deteriorated. In fact, more than half a century after the crash occurred, debate was rekindled after even more possibilities were put forward in a two-part investigation carried in a 1990 edition of the respected journal *Aeroplane Monthly*.

Some years after the accident a commemorative stone honouring the Duke of Kent and those killed with him was erected near the accident site. Here in Toronto the Princes' Gates serves as a lasting memorial to the other prince.

HERE'S WHERE YOU SERVED YOUR TIME

September 7, 1997

Central Prison looking west from Strachan Avenue.

One of the most frequent questions I'm asked is whether I've ever been at a loss for a story for this column, which, if I might say, has been appearing every Sunday now for more than 20 years. The answer to the question is simple: no. Our city has so much history that it's frequently more of a problem deciding which of the many stories to feature each week. Take, for instance, a story that came to me out of the blue while hosting a bus tour of the city a few months ago. I was approached by one of my guests, Myrtle Pike, who told me that her father, William Charles Hill, worked and lived at the old Central Prison, which stood on the west side of Strachan Avenue, north of the CNE grounds. He had been hired as a driver by the prison's third warden, Dr. John Gilmour. His father, and Myrtle's grandfather, Fred Hill, also worked there as a guard.

Myrtle was born at her uncle's place on Palmerston Avenue so her mother wouldn't have to tell her friends that her daughter was born in prison. During a follow-up visit with Myrtle and her husband in their Etobicoke home, I was shown one of the prison's ancient padlocks and an unusual key (of sufficient length to reach through the stone prison walls to the lock of the cell door), both of which were given to her father when the prison closed. I also inspected her father's revolver, which has since been turned over to Jack Webster, curator of the fascinating Metro Toronto Police Museum at 40 College Street.

Staff of Toronto's Central Prison. Guard Fred Hill is sixth from right (photo courtesy Myrtle Pike).

But I'm getting a little ahead of myself. I should really explain a little more about the old Central Prison. Most people are familiar (at least indirectly) with the Don Jail on Gerrard Street, the city's fourth jail, that opened for business in 1864. Central, to use the vernacular of the day, opened a decade later to take the overflow from the Don with the really bad eggs shipped off the penitentiary in Kingston. Its location in an unpopulated area on the city's western outskirts (the Town of Parkdale didn't amalgamate — there's that word again — with the city until 1889) was selected to permit expansion as necessary. The prison consisted of two cell houses, each four floors high, with a total of 600 cells. To help while away the time (as well as generate some income), there was a bakery, as well as five workshops where items such as brooms and lengths of rope were made by the inmates. For the unrepentant there were 16 underground dungeons.

A portion of the prison chapel still stands west of Strachan Avenue, 1997.

Prison padlock and key.

With the changing attitudes towards the treatment of the criminal element, Central Prison was abandoned in 1915, and inmates were moved to the new reformatory at Guelph or the jail farm at Lansing, south of Richmond Hill. By 1919, the Central Prison buildings were so much rubble except for a portion of the prison chapel, erected near the main building in 1877. It can still be seen standing forlornly at the far end of the large parking lot on the west side of Strachan south of Liberty Street. Incidentally, this latter thoroughfare got its name as it was the street upon which reformed prisoners set foot when they'd served their time.

** Not long after the marriage of Prince Charles to Diana Frances Spencer on July 29, 1981, I was chatting with Arthur Bousfield, the editor of *Monarchy in Canada*, a popular publication that documents the lives and times of the Queen and her family, past and present. During the course of our conversation I mentioned that I was busily researching material on the origins of Toronto street names and was amazed at the number that had royal connections.

And while Queen, King, and certainly the Queen Elizabeth Way have obvious royal connections — Queen Victoria, King George III, and the Queen Mother — I was somewhat surprised to find out from Arthur that the man for whom Toronto's Richmond Street was named is was a relative of Diana, the new Princess of Wales.

Arthur presented me with a family tree to prove his point. An examination of the tree reveals that Charles Lennox, fourth Duke of Richmond, the man who was appointed Governor-in-Chief of Canada in 1818, only served in that prestigious capacity until his untimely death on August 28, 1819, as a result of being bitten by a rabid fox. The duke died in a small cabin not far from the banks of the Rideau River. The present Town of Richmond, Ontario, located a few miles southwest of Ottawa and not far from that small cabin, was named years later to honour his memory.

Charles' son, who became the fifth Duke of Richmond on his father's death, fought against the armies of Napoleon at the Battle of Waterloo alongside Sir John Colborne (Colborne Street).

His daughter, Lady Cecilia, married George Charles Bingham, fourth Earl of Lucan. Their daughter, Rosalind, married James Hamilton, third Duke of Abercorn, in 1894, and their daughter, Lady Cynthia, married Albert Edward John, seventh Earl of Spencer (incidentally, a descendant of a daughter of King James II, who, among other things, was the second governor of the Hudson's Bay Company). The family seat was at Althorp, Northampton. The seventh Earl of Spencer was Diana's grandfather.

WHALE SIGHTING IN TORONTO

September 14, 1997

Wyland's "whaling wall" at Redpath Sugars, Queen's Quay East, 1997 (photo courtesy Richard Feltoe, curator of the Redpath Sugars museum).

For the past little while hundreds of curious spectators watched as mural artist Wyland (he used to have a first name, but no longer) created another of his trademark "whaling walls" on the north wall of the raw-sugar storage building at Redpath Sugars on Queen's Quay East at the foot of Jarvis Street. This work, measuring 31.5 m (97 ft) high and 47.5 m (146 ft.) wide would, in the space of one week, become mural #70 in the young artist's international quest that started in Laguna Beach, California, in 1981 to create 100 similar tributes that emphasize the importance of preserving ocean environments worldwide. Wyland's work has already become one of the feature attractions along the Waterfront Regeneration Trust sponsored Waterfront Trail, which follows the Lake Ontario shoreline and links 177 natural areas, 143 parks and promenades, 80 marinas and yacht clubs, and hundreds of historic attractions, fairs, museums, art galleries, and festivals.

While many viewers of Wyland's whales may think that his are the first of this species to appear in our city, history tells us that would be an incorrect assumption. Torontonians saw their very first whale more than a century ago. And like Wyland's it, too, was inanimate. In fact, it was dead.

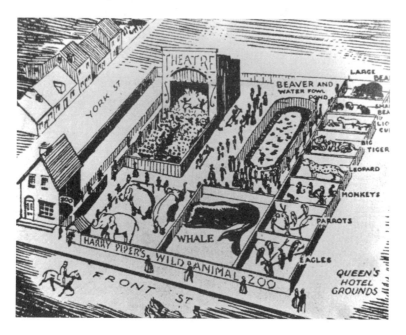

Bird's eye view of Harry Piper's Zoological Gardens, a site now occupied, in part, by the Royal York Hotel.

Brought to Toronto in hopes of enticing crowds to visit the city's first zoo, a privately owned enterprise run by Toronto born Harry Piper, this unfortunate mammal had been discovered after it washed ashore on one of Prince Edward Island's beautiful beaches. When Piper, whose small zoo on the north side of Front Street (about where the main entrance to the elegant Royal York Hotel is today) opened its doors to the public in 1880, got wind of the discovery the eager entrepreneur quickly approached his friendly bank manager and after some negotiating (who says banks aren't approachable), the bank official agreed to loan Harry $3 000. Piper then notified those who had found the whale and before the end of 1881 the 12-ton, 53-foot-long creature was on its way to Toronto ignominiously strapped onto two railway flat cars.

Once in the city, the rest of the mammal's journey was easy since the rail freight yards were just across Front Street from the zoo. That winter, Harry Piper's Zoological Gardens was constantly filled with spectators eager to view the whale. For an extra charge, visitors could have their picture taken standing in the deceased whale's propped-open jaw. As the seasons changed, and with the help of lots and lots of ice, the whale continued to attract huge crowds. However, before long there just wasn't enough ice, and the fast disintegrating carcass became more of a detraction than an attraction.

But, seeing the potential to squeeze a few more bucks out of what was left of the once exalted mammal, officials of the Toronto Industrial Exhibition (now the CNE) agreed to display what little remained during the annual fair of 1882. When the fair closed, what remained of the blubber and bones was removed to the wilds of High Park, where time and vandals took care of what was left. All but a chunk of whale backbone, that is, which someone had thrown into the harbour just across the street from the old zoo. Even back then some regarded the bay as nothing more than a large and convenient garbage can.

Almost a century later, when the tunnel for the TTC's new Harbourfront streetcar line was being built under Front and Bay streets, a member of the construction crew unearthed a bone identified as being part of a whale's vertebra. Local zoological experts were thrown into a tizzy. The presence of a saltwater mammal in this part of the world...impossible! Or was it? But the excitement quickly dissipated when the saga of Harry Piper's whale was recounted.

And while Harry Piper and his whale have long since departed, this flamboyant showman of yesteryear is still remembered in the name of little Piper Street, which runs west off York Street behind the gracious Royal York Hotel.

SHE WAS A MUSICAL SWEETHEART

September 28, 1997

March 21, 1947, newspaper ad for *The Jolson Story*, which was screened at two of the city's largest theatres, the Tivoli and the Eglinton.

I can't say enough good things about the stage production *Jolson, the Musical* presently being featured at Toronto's handsome Royal Alexandra Theatre. And while I'm certainly not a theatre critic I can describe *Jolson* as one of those exceptional plays that have audiences leaving the theatre happier than when they entered.

In my column of June 15 I described Al's numerous visits to our city, each time performing on the same stage on which *Jolson* is now being presented. Al was back again in 1947, in voice at least, when the motion picture *The Jolson Story* made its debut on the screens of two of the city's largest theatres, the Tivoli at the corner of Victoria and Richmond and the Eglinton. While the former theatre vanished long ago, the latter still survives, beautifully restored, on the north side of Eglinton Avenue just west of Avenue Road.

The movie reviewer for the old Toronto *Telegram* concluded that the movie, which starred the "previously unknown" Larry Parks acting the part of the grown-up Jolson (child actor Scotty Beckett plays a young Asa Yoelson) and lip-syncing Jolson's distinctive voice, "will make audiences happy" and "be a revelation to those who have never heard of Jolson. To those who remember when the man was on the heights the movie will bring back delightful memories."

Canadian-born Ruby Keeler.

In the movie Al's wife, his fourth, was identified as Julie Benson and played by actress Evelyn Keyes. (In *Jolson, the Musical*, Ruby is played by Sally Ann Triplett.) In real life (as opposed to "reel" life) Al's fourth wife was, in fact, Ruby Keeler. She had requested that her name not be used in the movie, having divorced Al in 1939. By the time the movie hit the silver screen Ruby had remarried and was not eager to be reminded of her 11 years with the egocentric Jolson. They were not happy days.

Interestingly, it was the 43-year-old Jolson's marriage to 19-year-old Ruby that presents us with another of Jolson's Canadian connections. Ruby, who would become a true Broadway and Hollywood star in her own right, was born in Dartmouth, Nova Scotia, on August 25, 1909, the daughter of a struggling Halifax truck driver. In an attempt to improve the family's lot in life, the impoverished father moved his family to New York City. From his meagre take-home pay, derived from delivering ice, the father managed to set aside a few pennies each week to pay for dancing lessons for young Ruby. In true fairy-story fashion, the youngster's hard work paid off when she was "discovered" by the great Florenz Ziegfield. Bit parts, then starring roles in several Broadway musicals followed. Then it was off to Hollywood where Ruby and Dick Powell became screen favourites in such films as *Forty-Second Street*, *Gold Diggers of 1933*, and *Footlight Parade*.

Ruby starred in her last film in 1941 (*Sweetheart of the Campus*), and though she had some misgivings made a successful comeback in 1971 starring, at the age of 60, in a total of 871 performances of the revival of *No No Nanette*. Several of those performances were at Toronto's O'Keefe (now Hummingbird) Centre.

Ruby Keeler died on February 28, 1993.

THE LAUGH'S ON US

October 5, 1997

As I read the obituaries documenting the life and times of the late Red Skelton in the local and international newspapers I was saddened not simply because the world had lost one of its great clowns (and a favourite of mine), but because nowhere in those articles was the story describing how Red actually got his start in show business revealed. And while I realize how inappropriate it is to speak for the departed, I'm sure that Red too would have been disappointed to learn that Canada, where his earliest successes occurred, wasn't even mentioned.

To be sure there was an oblique reference in the *New York Times* to Skelton's appearance in the mid-1930s at the Loew's Princess Theatre in Montreal, but no where is our city mentioned. Having met and chatted with the man on a number of occasions during his O'Keefe Centre and Roy Thomson Hall visits (Red also appeared at the CNE grandstand), I know that the omission would have hurt him. He was especially touched when then Mayor Art Eggleton declared the day of the comic's 1989 visit "Red Skelton Day."

Richard Red Skelton (there were no quotation marks around his middle name) was born on July 18, 1913, in Vincennes, Indiana, into a fatherless family, Joe Skelton having died two months prior to Red's arrival. By the time the youngster was seven he was selling newspapers, with the small income helping to support his mother, Ida Mae, and his three older brothers. It didn't take long for Red to discover that sassing potential customers quickly turned them into real customers just so they could get rid of him.

Several years later Red joined a medicine show where he developed the art of the pratfall. His frequent falls to get a laugh from his audience resulted in severe ligament damage that was to cause the clown great pain in his later years. I recall that while chatting with him after his most recent appearance in Toronto he volunteered that the pain in his knees was so severe during the show that he was almost sick to his stomach on stage. He said he was going to get the problem looked at. I don't believe he ever did.

By the time the rusty-haired comic was 14 he had gained considerable experience, having performed in a number of small-town vaudeville houses and on the riverboat *Cotton Blossom* (coincidentally the show boat in *Show Boat*) that plied the Mississippi River. By the time he was 20 he had tried the movies, which had just gotten their voice, but his success on the silver screen (or more likely a stretched bedsheet) was less than remarkable. That talent would have to wait another few years before being recognized.

Red got billing as The Clown Prince in this August 28, 1936 ad for Shea's Hippodrome on Bay Street.

In the meantime, Red latched onto a vaudeville circuit that frequently ventured north of the border and before long was performing his comedy routine in front of audiences at the Loew's Princess in Montreal. Then, catching the inter-city train, the next week would see him convulsing crowds at Shea's Hippodrome on Bay Street here in Toronto.

Following a 1936 appearance at Loew's in Montreal, Red and the rest of the troupe wait for the Toronto train. That's Red, back row centre.
(photo courtesy Jeanette Heller)

Red's first Toronto appearance was at Shea's on September 1, 1936, when he was a minor part of a program that featured the comedy team of Tom Howard and George Shelton "direct from the Rudy Vallee radio show." While Red was on the same bill he wasn't identified in any ads until a few days after the show had opened, and then simply as Red Skelton, the Clown Prince.

Then it was back to Montreal. Ten days later, Red was back in Toronto ("by popular demand," according to the ads), and this time received more prominent billing as both "Your Favourite Master of Ceremonies" and "The Red-Head Madcap of Comedy." This time the headliner was John Bowles, "the Screen's Greatest Romantic Singing Star," who crooned such 1936 hits as "Waiting at the Gate for Katie," "One Alone," and "Rose of the Rancho." Red also shared the stage with Nell Kelly and Her Drum, acrobatic dancer Marjorie Palm, plus Rosamund with her accordion and Gordon's Comedy Canines.

In reviewing the show, the Toronto *Evening Telegram* newspaper described Red's act in the following terms:

"Red Skelton, red-haired, rubber-faced master of ceremonies is the main driving force and chief laugh getter of the show. He knocked them in the aisles earlier this month and is back with a whole new routine of gags and clowning. He is the perfect clown...his foolishness is refreshing and completely contagious."

Never has a stage review been more prophetic.

Skelton's career continued to develop on the two Canadian theatre stages until one day early in 1937 when the 24-year-old decided to try his luck south of the border. The Capital Theatre in Washington, D.C., was the chosen location. On the theatre marquee were the words "The Canadian Comedian, Red Skelton."

Red was always a fan of Canada and especially of our city. He confided to me that his "doughnut dunker" was born during one of his Montreal appearances while the "mean widdle kid" had come to him during a visit to our Exhibition.

Recently I spoke with Red's friend and promoter Tom Kalyn, who confirmed that comic's last public appearance was in October, 1994, right here in Toronto, the very place he got his start 58 years earlier. He suggested that Red would have found that totally appropriate.

Red, the world was a better place thanks to you and a sadder one now that you're gone.

ROADS TOOK THEIR TOLL IN EARLY T.O.

October 12, 1997

T hose electronic gadgets called transponders that are suspended over Highway 407 may be new as is the highway itself, but there's one thing for certain, the idea of toll roads is as old as Toronto. In fact, there's a good chance that the concept of paying to use Yonge Street predates the community's name change from York to the present Toronto by more than a dozen years. Even the reason for creating a toll road back in the early 1800s mimics the reason for making 407 a toll road. Those using the road should be the ones to pay for its construction and upkeep. In 1820, lower Yonge Street was a mess, in fact it was nothing more than a path cleared through the forest that surrounded the original townsite that had come into being further east.

To provide the funds necessary to keep the road in some sort of repair, a toll was levied on those whose wagons used the path, and a toll-collecting both was erected at the corner of Yonge and King streets. Actually, to call it a corner is a misnomer since at that time in our city's history the now bustling intersection was really not much more than the crossing of two narrow, dusty (or muddy, depending on the time of year) paths. This toll booth was referred to as the first, as there was a second farther north, at the present intersection of College and Carlton streets.

As time went on and the maintenance of the community's main drag became more and more of a challenge with the ever increasing numbers of wagons, additional collection points were erected. The Village of Yorkville gate stood in the middle of Yonge Street at the village's southern boundary (now Bloor Street) and was fitted with both a turnstile and a gate that barred pedestrians, animals, and vehicles until the appropriate toll was forthcoming. While the rates for the earliest days have yet to be discovered, suffice it to say that they wouldn't be far off the 1875 figures: passage of one pig, goat, or sheep, one cent, rising to a maximum of ten cents for a loaded wagon pulled by a pair of horses.

Over the next few years the location of the Yorkville gate moved north until by 1870 it was located at the top of what was known as Gallows Hill (near the CHUM radio studio). The hill got this rather gruesome title not because hangings took place there, but rather thanks to a huge tree on the side of the road that had partially toppled, creating, from a distance and especially on moonlit nights, the appearance of a gallows.

The Rebecca Street sign near the Queen and Ossington intersection hints at the tollgate that stood at that corner years earlier.

Other gates controlled animal and vehicle passage all along Yonge Street and well out into the countryside including several near the farming communities of Thornhill and Aurora. It's not hard to imagine the animosity that these gates generated resulting in more than a few disagreements as riders and farmers alike tried to run the gate.

A link with Toronto's ancient tollgates can still be found on Queen Street West. For a time there was a tollgate at the south end of Dundas Street at its intersection with Queen. (Originally Ossington Avenue between Queen and Dundas was the southerly extension of Dundas Street.) This gate was the site of many altercations, many of which involved a merchant taking firewood to the garrison at Fort York. Believing he was exempt from tolls, he began avoiding the gate, using a shortcut through the woods east of the troublesome intersection, a path that evolved into today's Rebecca Street. The thoroughfare took its name from the Rebeccaites, who systematically destroyed the tollgates in south Wales in 1843. They in turn had taken their name from comments concerning Rebekah in the Bible (*Genesis* xxiv: 60).

The last tollgates in York County vanished in 1896, following the signing of an agreement by both city and county officials that permitted county residents to obtain space in the St. Lawrence Market for the sale of their goods at no charge.

Though the last of the Toronto area tollgates vanished more than a century ago there have been several attempts in recent years to resurrect them in a different form. In 1952 then Mayor Allan Lamport recommended that the new cross-waterfront superhighway, later to be renamed the Gardiner Expressway, be constructed as a toll road with a fee paid for every vehicle entering the city limits.

Interestingly, toll gates did reappear with the opening of the new Highway 407 on June 7, 1997.

The Yorkville Toll Gate, Yonge Street near Cottingham Avenue, c. 1865

CRUISE SHIP REVIVAL ON GREAT LAKES

October 19, 1997

I t was exactly one month ago today that the first cruise ship in many a year called at the Port of Toronto. The motor vessel (MV) *Columbus* of the Hapag-Lloyd line is scheduled to return to Toronto today as her inaugural season of Great Lakes cruising comes to an end. And if all goes as expected, *Columbus* and perhaps other cruise ships will be back on the Great Lakes again next summer.

Prior to the arrival of *Columbus* in Toronto on September 19, the last time a cruise ship sailed into the harbour was in 1975, when a vessel called *Discoverer* made an unsuccessful attempt to revive the Great Lakes cruise business.

MV *Columbus* arrives in Toronto, September 19, 1997. (Toronto *Sun* photo)

I have deliberately used the term "revive" since the art of cruising the Great Lakes is nothing new. It was an extremely popular pastime that flourished during the first half of this century. In fact, cruises were popular as late as 1967 when the *North American* and *South American*, a pair of large passenger ships of the Chicago, Duluth and Georgian Bay Transit Company that had offered seven-day cruises between the ports of Detroit and Duluth as well as between Detroit, Montreal, and the Saguenay region for nearly half a century, returned to the lakes with cruises to the Expo '67 site in Montreal.

Closer to home, many readers will remember the *Keewatin* and *Assiniboia*, which operated cruises between Port McNicoll on Georgian Bay and the Canadian lakehead. Picture postcards abound showing these two beautiful CPR ships, which entered service in the early 1900s and lasted well into the 1960s, moored alongside the Toronto trains at the flower-bedecked Port McNicoll dock. *Assiniboia* was scrapped while *Keewatin* lives on as a museum ship in Douglas, Michigan.

Many U.S. Great Lakes cities were home ports to cruise ships, perhaps the best known locally being the *Canadiana*, which operated for years between Buffalo and the popular Crystal Beach amusement park across the lake near Fort Erie. There were tentative plans to restore the old craft, which, having been retired, was towed to Port Colborne and moored not far from where Toronto's Island ferry *Trillium* was rebuilt 21 years ago. I believe those plans are now dead.

The roster of other popular American passenger cruise boats of yesteryear would include the mammoth sidewheelers *Greater Detroit* and *Greater Buffalo*, which ran between their namesake cities. Built in 1924, both vessels were larger in all respects than the modern MV *Columbus*, and carried more passengers.

An artist's impressionistic view of four of the most popular Great Lakes cruise ships racing towards Toronto, c 1910.

Here in Toronto there was a time when the bay was dotted with all sorts of passenger steamers setting out or returning from day trips to the various Niagara Peninsula ports or overnight cruises to far distant points such as Rochester (the city being inland, Rochester's port was nearby Olcott Beach), Kingston and the Thousand Islands. The steamers *Kingston* and *Toronto* were popular on the latter routes. Other larger vessels would continue downriver to Montreal or perhaps even as far as Quebec City. This latter excursion was particularly thrilling with vessels such as the *Rapids King*, *Rapids Queen*, or *Rapids Prince* running the Lachine Rapids on the St. Lawrence River. Visitors to Ward's Island can still see the hull of the old *Rapids Queen* beached in front of the Queen City Yacht Club where it acts as a breakwater protecting the club beach from often vicious cross-bay storms. Occasionally, vessels usually seen only on the upper Great Lakes would call at the Port of Toronto. And when they did, handsome ships like the ill-fated sisters *Hamonic* and *Noronic* would cause quite a flurry as thousands flocked to the waterfront to welcome them to town.

On Toronto Bay, the aptly named Niagara boats became legendary with the *Dalhousie City* and *Northumberland* carrying thousands of fun- and sun-seeking Torontonians to and from the amusement park at Port Dalhousie on the south side of the lake where, in the summertime, the nickel merry-go-round still twirls. The community is now a suburb of St. Catharines.

Other Niagara bound boats included *Coronna*, *Cibola*, *Chicora*, and *Chippewa*, but without question the most popular was *Cayuga*, which operated, virtually without negative incident, from 1907 until she was retired from service in 1957 and scrapped four years later. Remnants of *Cayuga* can be found at the Marine Museum in Exhibition Place.

By the way, whenever you read about the possible inauguration of a new commuter service between Hamilton and Toronto, remember that *Macassa*, *Modjeska*, as well as the revolutionary *Turbinia*, the first turbine-powered vessel and the fastest passenger craft on the Great Lakes, were doing just that nearly a century ago.

RAISE A GLASS TO THE SILVER RAIL

October 26, 1997

Today when we talk about city landmarks (and I use the term "city" in post-amalgamation context) we usually think of such modern structures as the CN Tower, Viljo Revell's striking City Hall on Queen Street, or SkyDome. Or perhaps historic buildings like Montgomery's Inn on Dundas Street West, Gibson House on north Yonge Street, or the partially restored Lambton Tavern near the Humber River come to mind. And then there are natural wonders like the Scarborough Bluffs and the valley of the Don. And some may think of the Silver Rail at the Yonge and Shuter corner. Now, some may say that the latter doesn't fit the landmark mould, but for many Torontonians the Silver Rail is as much part of the city's history as the Princes' Gates. In recognition of the Silver Rail's place in our city's history, a commemorative plaque was recently bestowed on this popular dining establishment by Heritage Toronto (the new name of the Toronto Historical Board).

Now, while it's true that Toronto has many fine and long-established eateries, what makes the Silver Rail so special for many citizens is the fact that it was one of the first establishments in the entire province in which they could enjoy a glass of spirits (read "liquor") either with a meal or all by itself, and legally to boot.

That may not sound like much in the freewheeling 1990s (heck, soon you'll be able to buy booze even on a Sunday), but a little more than 50 years ago the concept of going into a tavern, hotel or club and having a rye and water or gin and tonic was unheard of in staid old Ontario. Sure, the consumption of a glass of beer or wine with a meal or even a glass of beer by itself (but not wine) had been approved in 1934, but with the passage of the Ontario Liquor Licence Act in 1946 you could even a glass of spirits, and you could have it with or without food.

Even so, liquor remained such a touchy subject that the year after, the premier of the province was defeated by "Temperance Bill" Temple, who campaigned in the High Park riding almost exclusively on an anti-drink platform. The repercussions of Temple's beliefs are still being felt in that part of our planet.

That's not to say that the passage of this act eliminated all the draconian restraints. No siree! Rules still governed not only the decor of the room, but the wearing apparel of the staff along with a hundred and one other things.

We're Number One! On April 1, 1947, the Barclay Hotel on Front Street West, at Simcoe, became the first place in the city to serve spirits following the passage of new liquor laws the previous year.

When the new act came into force a total of 77 outlets throughout the province had been awarded a lounge licence (spirits, wine and beer by the glass, no food), a dining lounge licence (the same drinks with or without food), a dining room licence (the same drinks but only with food), a PHM licence, or a PHMW licence. The latter allowed public houses to serve only beer. In the first instance it could be served to men only, and in the second to men and women. (Boy, wouldn't the equal rights people have a field day with those rules today?)

Of the 77 approved locations, Toronto had 40, including places like the Albany Club, the Embassy Tavern, the Walker House, Windsor Arms, Winston Theatre Grill, Hotel Manitou, and Pierson's Hotel (both on the Island), the Prince George Hotel and, of course, the Royal York.

Now, while the Silver Rail may have been the place many Torontonians had that historic first hard drink, it was not, as some continue to believe, the first city establishment to offer liquor with or without a meal. That honour goes to the now demolished Hotel Barclay, which stood at the northeast corner of Front and Simcoe streets. And the reason is quite simple. When the government licences were issued, the permit holders found it necessary to train bar staff in the lost technique of mixing drinks, all kinds of drinks. The Barclay, on the other hand, got the jump on them all by bringing in experienced staff from south of the border. As a result, the hotel was able to open on the day the law took effect, April 1, 1947. The Silver Rail was next, opening its doors at noon the following day to a line of customers that stretched along Shuter as far as Victoria. Many in that line had been standing in the pouring rain for more than an hour. Others to open on April 2 were the Club Norman (Adelaide treet East) and the Metropole Hotel (southwest corner of King and York).

Prices for "highballs ranged from 45¢ to $1.60. Beer was 21¢ a bottle at the bar and 35¢ a glass in the dining lounge. But a problem was looming on the horizon. The Wartime Prices Board was keeping a tight control on the availability of sugar, and many felt that it wouldn't be long before the price of mixed drinks would have to be increased. Boy, did they have that right.

GROWING UP WITH CANADIAN TIRE

November 2, 1997

When I was a kid going to high school I was lucky enough to have a car. Well, I didn't exactly have a car. Phil Lewis, my boss at the drugstore where I legally peddled drugs (on my bike), and his wife, Joan, had a second car, which they would let me drive. It was a little green and white 1954 Nash Metropolitan convertible, to be sure a collector's car today, but back in the late 1950s it was simply a way for me to get from here to there and, with a bit of luck, back again.

Then, after accumulating a few hundred dollars during the summer holidays, I moved up in the world and bought a used 1958 Hillman Minx from Harry Norman who, with Jan Wietzes, ran the Lilliputian Supertest gas station that occupied the northeast corner of Mt. Pleasant Road and Broadway Avenue. Jan's boys now operate the Wietzes Toyota dealership on north Yonge Street.

Oh, I almost forgot. For short time I also owned a 1949 Morris Minor, something that with the passage of time would also be termed a collectible and qualify for the special $19 licensing fee. Today I remember this vehicle with a shudder since it came equipped with mechanical brakes that gave it a stopping distance just a few feet shorter than that of the old Peter Witt streetcars. In fact, you had to plan when you were going to apply the brakes even before leaving the house.

The entrance to 839 Yonge Street is visible to the right of the northbound Peter Witt train on the Yonge route, 1942.

The salvation for those of us with tired old cars was the local Canadian Tire store. I probably spent as much time in the Yonge and Church street store as I did in school. Every few days I'd roam the store's narrow aisles, carefully navigating the slanted concrete floors, then wait while the guy on roller skates retrieved my order for an old-fashioned canister-type oil filter, or a set of ignition points, rotor and condenser, or a tin of chrome polish (what's chrome? today's kids ask). Then there was the time I bought a couple of containers of gold spray paint with which I would convert my so-so chrome hubcaps to flashy gold ones. A couple of days later one cap went flying off, shot across the asphalt and into a farm field on the west side of Kennedy Road north of Sheppard. I often wondered whether the person who found that gold hubcap thought he'd struck a precious mother lode.

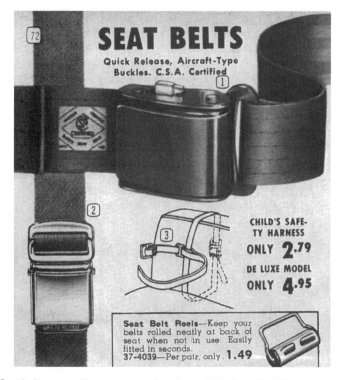

Seat belts were still an accessory item in the 1966 Canadian Tire catalogue.

I even remember buying seat belts and a spring-loaded retractor gizmo for my Hillman years before they became standard equipment. (Anyone know where I can buy a couple of pair for my 1955 Pontiac?) My car had another safety accessory that has recently been reintroduced. It was a small light that was affixed somewhere in the grill and wired into the system so that it would only be illuminated when the ignition was on. Today, these things are identified as daytime running lights and while standard here in Canada are now just being introduced in the States.

"FOOEY-FACE"

. . . **Gives the bird to the Horn blowing Nuisance!**

. . . **Tongue Sticks Out!**

. . . **Eyes Illuminate!**

. . . **Gives out a Razzing Sound!**

The answer to the motorist's prayers! An effective come-back to the horn blowing pest. Control mounts on steering column and when pressed, tongue sticks out, eyes flash and figure gives out a razzing sound. Easily installed in a few minutes. Figure size 6" x 5" finished in 3 colors.

There's never been an item like FOOEY-FACE . . . it has taken the U.S. market by storm. Exclusive sale in Canada.
Price Complete **$2.89**

One accessory I didn't buy, a "Fooey-Face," which, affixed to your licence plate, gave "the bird to the horn blowing nuisance" behind your car.

In the mid-1960s there were 14 Canadian Tire Corporation stores in the Metro area (today there are 25). But for me the old store on Yonge just north of Davenport was the closest. And when I describe it as old I'm not exaggerating. It had actually been built decades earlier to house something called the Grand Central Market, a sort of uptown version of the St. Lawrence Market.

That ideal failed and in 1937 the founders of Canadian Tire, brothers John William and Alfred Jackson Billes, who had started the whole thing back in the fall of 1922 in a small garage across the street from the Don Jail on Gerrard Street East, moved in. The business was called the Hamilton Tire and Rubber Company (Hamilton not for the city, but the nearby side street).

The boys' automotive parts business grew quickly, necessitating moves to larger and larger stores, the first at 639 Yonge, northeast corner of Isabella, then across Isabella to 625–637 Yonge, then on to the abandoned market building a few blocks up the street.

Over the ensuing years additional associate stores opened throughout the province, each operated by what the corporation referred to as an associate dealer. By the time I was to adopt the Yonge Street store, Fred, AJ's son, was the associate dealer, a position he held until 1988 when the present dealer, Ken Mann, took over. Ken had done time in Canadian Tire stores in Fredericton, New Brunswick (30 years) and Oshawa, Ontario (17 years). Ken was also in charge when the shiny, new store, just steps north of the old one, opened in 1989. A good chunk of the original 839 was kept and fixed up, and is now used for special displays.

Originally, the Billes boys stuck pretty much to basic car parts — batteries, tires, mufflers, and the like. Today, as Canadian Tire celebrates its 75th birthday, the corporation's 428 stores, coast to coast, feature not only automotive products, but gardening supplies, sporting goods, and housewares, as well.

IT'S A RIGHT ROYAL ANNIVERSARY

November 9, 1997

This year marks the 75th anniversary of a long-time Toronto tradition, the Royal Agricultural Winter Fair. But if things had gone just a little smoother for its founders, 1997 would actually be the fair's 76th birthday and all the planned anniversary hoopla would have taken place last year. What happened, you may well ask. I'll get to that in a moment, but first let's look at why there's a Royal at all.

In the early years of this century Canada was a much more rural nation than it is today, and as such a great deal of time and effort was placed on the improvement of the quality of the country's livestock herds, field crops, and the calibre of its horticulture and floriculture. Others eagerly sought out the latest dairy techniques and ways to improve their poultry interests.

Mayor Tommy Church lays cornerstone for the city's new
Coliseum on July 26, 1921.

To be sure, one way to keep on top of the latest news was to attend farm-oriented trade shows like the Winter Fair held for years in Guelph, Ontario, or the big agricultural show in Chicago. In an attempt to bring together Canada's farming community a National Live Stock, Horticulture and Dairy Show was held in November, 1913, in several of the old livestock buildings at the east end of Toronto's Exhibition Park. Unfortunately, the outbreak of the Great War the following summer resulted in this show becoming a one-time event. Nevertheless, the die had been cast, and when hostilities finally ended on November 11, 1918, plans were quickly revived to develop a truly national winter fair.

Before long meetings involving interested and influential people were being held. Soon all the necessary elements for the establishment of an all Canadian winter fair were in place, concluding with a meeting in Hamilton on October 28, 1919, at which time Toronto was selected as the site of a national winter fair.

Actually, the site selection was close, with Hamilton losing out by a single tie-breaking vote cast by William Dryden. No doubt Toronto's unmatched offer to erect a million-dollar structure in which to hold the fair did much to swing the vote.

Less than a month later the Agricultural Winter Fair Association of Canada would receive its charter with the title amended slightly on February 19, 1920, when permission was granted by none other than King George V to have "Royal" added to the title. With that slight but important modification, the Royal Agricultural Winter Fair was born. And now it was on with the show!

First, however, it would be necessary to take the City of Toronto up on its generous offer to erect a new $1-million building in which the proposed fair could be held. Working in concert with members of the Royal Winter Fair Association, city architect G.F.W. Price designed what was at first simply called the Live Stock Arena. Ground was broken for the new building on June 7, 1921, and the cornerstone was laid with appropriate ceremony by Mayor Tommy Church on July 26.

Just 128 working days after construction began the building contractor placed an ad in the local newspapers stating the "Million Dollar Live Stock Building" was ready for occupancy.

But something was missing. Facilities to properly heat the building were nowhere near ready. So while prize lists, catalogues, and other promotional material had been prepared, the directors found it necessary to postpone the opening of the inaugural Royal Agricultural Winter Fair, which had been scheduled to open on November 16, 1921.

Everyone felt it was too much of a gamble to hold an entertaining show in a building that was too cold. Bad press and unhappy visitors could ruin everything. In addition, concerns over the health and welfare of show animals also led to the fair's cancellation.

The new building was finally ready for the December 16, 1921, opening of a mammoth athletic program sponsored by the Sportsmen's Patriotic Association. Once again Mayor Church officiated. Many other events took place in the new building until finally, on November 22, 1922, the Royal Agricultural Winter Fair got its chance.

To describe the first Royal as a success would be a definite understatement. A first-year attendance in excess of 150 000 exceeded all expectations, as did the number of entries in the various classes — 1 850 horses, 2 500 head of cattle, 9 100 chickens and roosters, 900 sheep, 700 swine, and exactly 436 foxes. Displays of dairy products, fruits, flowers, vegetables, and seeds were enormous in quantity and pleasantly surprising in quality.

As one visitor summed up the first edition of the Royal, "this fair is better than the one in Chicago." Quite a compliment for a event that almost didn't happen.

PEOPLE POWER SAVES STREETCARS

November 16, 1997

Picture Toronto without its old City Hall at the corner of Queen and Bay streets. Or what about a Toronto without a fleet of ferryboats running to and from the Island or barren of its impressive-looking police officers astride beautiful big horses? And what would Toronto be without streetcars gliding along downtown streets?

The Hawker-Siddeley people sketched this concept for the new Toronto streetcar one month before the TTC officially decided to retain this type of transit vehicle. Note old and new City Halls in the background and the route and destination signs reading an impossible combination, Queen–Danforth.

For many of us these features are a few of the things that make Toronto the place in which we want to live. Amazingly, however, a glimpse into our city's past reveals that at one time or another each of these features, which together help make Toronto truly unique, has faced potential elimination. Fortunately, people power ensured that all are still very much with us.

Let's take a closer look at one of these events, the one with which I became personally involved through a citizens' group called Streetcars for Toronto.

In the fall of 1972 (can it really be 25 years ago?) TTC staff submitted a report that recommended the elimination of all surface streetcar operations in Toronto starting with the immediate replacement of the streetcars on the Mt. Pleasant leg of the St. Clair line with trolley buses, followed by the conversion of the rest of the route to similar equipment. Following the full implementation of the plan, Toronto would join the ranks of most other large North American cities, all of which, at one time or another, had large fleets of streetcars. Picture it, Toronto without its streetcars.

The provincially sponsored Urban Transportation Development Corporation had a full-size wooden mock-up of it concept of Toronto's new streetcar on public display at the 1975 CNE. In this view the vehicle is on its way to the TTC Hillcrest Shop at the conclusion of the fair.

In defence of the staff's radical recommendation it must be recognized that the TTC, having failed to make provision for the future of its streetcar fleet and ancillary equipment, had backed itself into a corner. Most of the PCC Streamliners in the fleet were fast approaching the end of the line even though extensive rebuilding had given some of the vehicles a short stay of execution. Nevertheless, without replacement vehicles or comprehensive track and electrical overhead rehabilitation projects on the books, streetcar fleet abandonment was the only responsible recommendation possible.

This advice was given in spite of the fact that many staff felt the streetcar was still a much better people mover than a bus. In fact, Jim Kearns, the TTC's knowledgeable general manager, had often declared that "pound for pound, the streetcar is the best transit vehicle ever produced." He defended his staff's report in the simplest of terms: "It is now a simple matter of economics."

The new streetcar, known officially as the Canadian Light Rail Vehicle (CLRV), entered regular service on the 507 Long Branch route September 30, 1979. Official ceremonies welcoming the first of the 196 CLRVs took place the previous day at the Humber Loop. Here Etobicoke Mayor Dennis Flynn cuts the obligatory ribbon as TTC Chief General Manager Michael Warren (behind Flynn), Ontario Transportation Minister Jim Snow (left), and TTC Chairman Julian Porter (right) observe the ritual.

With the future of the streetcar looking very dim indeed, a small group of people (including me) quickly got together at the home of Paul Pickett (then alderman for Ward 10 and now a provincial court judge) one Saturday, and the group Streetcars for Toronto was born.

A detailed report outlining the innumerable virtues of the electric streetcar (including its place in Toronto's history) was speedily compiled (time was of the essence) and presented to the TTC Commissioners for their perusal. At the November 7, 1972, meeting the Commissioners rejected the recommendation to terminate all streetcar service in Toronto (except for the Rogers Road and Mt. Pleasant streetcar routes, which would end in the summer of 1975 and 1976, respectively) and instead requested that staff seek out an existing replacement vehicle. They went even further stating that, if necessary, Canadian companies should be contacted with a view to developing a brand new type of electric streetcar.

This the staff did and (to cut a very long and detailed story short) on September 30, 1979, the first of the new CLRVs — short for Canadian Light Rail Vehicle, a fancy name for a streetcar — went into service on the 507 (Long Branch) route. Before long, 196 of the new streetcars were roaming various streetcar routes.

Nine years later, July 17, 1988, the first of 52 Articulated Light Rail Vehicles (a larger version of the CLRV) began regular service on one of the city's busiest streetcar routes, 511 (Bathurst). The 501 (Queen) route saw the ALRVs on January 23, 1989.

Now there was absolutely no doubt that Toronto would remain a streetcar city!

Incidentally, in 1973 the Streetcars for Toronto Committee proposed the return of streetcars to Spadina Avenue. Another twenty-four years went by before the streetcar returned to Spadina.

MUSIC MAN OF THE CANADIAN ARMY

November 23, 1997

S everal weeks ago I was fortunate enough to attend a small welcome-home party for one of the world's most accomplished musicians, a Canadian far better known in distant countries than here at home. This man has done it all, written catchy pop tunes and composed stirring military marches and delicate symphonic suites. He's even written and arranged music for the silver screen. Over the years he's directed large orchestras and swinging dance bands, and closer to home even spent a half dozen years as an original on CBC's most popular radio variety show ever.

Canada's Robert Farnon.

Robert Farnon was born in 1917 here in Toronto (96 Woodside Avenue in the city's west end, to be precise) and at the age of 11 was introduced to the local music buffs as something of a wonder child exhibiting an amazing dexterity on a variety of instruments. After leaving nearby Humberside Collegiate Farnon, an accomplished trumpeter, began appearing with the orchestras of Percy Faith (another Toronto boy) and Geoffrey Waddington. In 1937 he became a charter member of the CBC's incredibly popular *Happy Gang* show, and a year later, at the age of 21, he wrote his first symphonic work, which was first performed by the Toronto Symphony Orchestra and later by Eugene Ormandy's prestigious Philadelphia Orchestra.

The war in Europe was in its fourth year when the young musician enlisted with the Canadian Army. As Captain Farnon he assembled an orchestra for *The Army Show*, a travelling revue-type production the government had created to promote recruitment into the armed forces.

In early 1944, as the invasion of Europe drew closer, Supreme Allied Commander General Dwight Eisenhower came up with a plan to give the allied troops news and entertainment over their own special radio network. One of the most popular shows to air on the new network was the Allied Expeditionary Forces Programme, featuring music presented by American and British bands conducted by Captain Glenn Miller and Sergeant George Melachrino, plus a Canadian segment led by our own Captain Bob Farnon, who had only recently been reassigned from his Canadian posting. Members of that group included the now legendary Murray Ginsberg, Teddy Roderman, Denny Vaughan, and a very young future TV personality, Fred Davis. On the evening of December 15, 1944, as the British and Canadian bands went on the air from studios in London, the planned hookup with Captain Miller's band, assembled in a Paris studio, was unexplainedly delayed. The Canadian and British bands kept filling in until it became obvious that something had happened to prevent Captain Miller's arrival at the Paris studio. Eventually Bob Farnon, and the world, learned what had happened. The Canadian built Norseman aircraft ferrying Captain Glenn Miller and two others to Paris from the tiny Twinwood Farm airfield near Bedford, England, had disappeared over the English Channel. Miller was never seen again.

Farnon continued to entertain troops and citizens alike with radio shows such as the *Canada Show*, the *Canada Guest Show*, and the *Canada Swing Show*. He and his band also made personal appearances at hospitals and army camps throughout Britain.

With little or no film, recording or television work available in Canada after the war, Farnon stayed in Great Britain where, in addition to conducting orchestras throughout Europe, he wrote, arranged, and conducted music for such stars as Frank Sinatra, Tony Bennett, and Vera Lynn.

Today, Robert Farnon, a perfect candidate for the Order of Canada, lives in the Channel Islands.

Recently, some of the lost recordings of Captain Bob Farnon and the Canadian Band of the Allied Expeditionary Force have been discovered, cleaned up, and put on a compact disc titled *The Lost Recordings*.

Not long after this column appeared, Robert Farnon was finally awarded the Order of Canada.

PART OF OUR PAST DISTILLED THROUGH FLATIRON BUILDING

November 30, 1997

Often, as I make my way along Front Street to the Sun Building during the more pleasant months of the year, I come across an idling tour bus that has just disgorged its complement of visitors to our city near the Jarvis and Front Street intersection. There they stand, video and still cameras capturing on tape or film one of the most intriguing vistas of our great city. From this vantage point the shiny new buildings lining Toronto's Bay Street business corridor seem to loom over a diminutive but still proud wedge-shaped office building at the intersection of Front, Wellington, and Church streets. The distinctive structure remains as a fragment of history reminding those who wish to know of a time when Toronto's original business district was located well to the east of Bay Street.

For our visitors, however, the driver's words prod them on. "Please get your picture then get back on the bus. The next stop on our tour will be ..." I often wonder what they tell their friends back home when they describe their vacation pictures. Especially the ones showing that funny old building in downtown Toronto.

Unfortunately, our guests have left, so I can't tell them the building's history. In fact, even most locals aren't aware that the building was created in 1891 and 1892 as a kind of an advertisement for the various types of liquor turned out by the extremely successful Gooderham and Worts Distilling Company, the largest in the nation and one of Toronto's most important businesses. Not that the building was meant to look like a bottle or anything like that, but rather its distinctive appearance at the busy intersection would become a kind of logo for the company and, not coincidentally, its many fine products.

The location of the new building, on a piece of land the surveyors refer to as a *gore*, had an added benefit. From his office's curved glass window on the top floor at the east apex of the triangle-shaped structure, company president (and son of the founder) George Gooderham could keep a watchful eye on the distillery complex just a few blocks to the southeast. Any changes in the factory's smoke or steam patterns or a slowing down in the ins and outs of the delivery wagons would result in a quick telephone call from the concerned boss.

In the early 1950s the Gooderham Building was still one of the city's larger office buildings. Note the two-way traffic on both Front (left) and Wellington streets.
(photo City of Toronto Archives)

Toronto Sketches 6

The same view in 1997. Though dwarfed by the city's new office towers, the old building still holds its head high.

Today, because of its obvious resemblance to a pressing iron, many simply refer to this city landmark as the flatiron building. And while the once-great Gooderham and Worts empire no longer operates the distillery, nor do they have offices in the old building, the structure is still officially known as the Gooderham Building, a fact confirmed by the name carved in the stone over the main entrance on Wellington Street.

MEMORIES OF CHRISTMAS PAST

December 21, 1997

Winters seemed to be colder back when I was a kid. Anyone else remember when the milk use to freeze after the milkman left it on the porch? I can hear the kids now... "What's a milkman?"

Last year in this column, I described a few of my earliest memories of Christmases past as I was growing up in a much less sophisticated Toronto. One of those memories, the annual trip to Eaton's Toyland, struck an especially sensitive chord with many of my readers. Many recalled with fondness Santa's Northland Castle ("Santa Snaps" — 2 for 25¢), the incredibly talented Toyland magician Johnny Giordamane, "Topsy Turvey Town," Toto the clown, and the Toyland Treasure Train, described as "a really, really train with a puffy engine modelled after a full-size CNR passenger train. Climb aboard and travel through the Rocky Mountains and find a surprise package at the end! Tickets, 25¢ each". It didn't mean anything to me then, but it I have since discovered that the locomotive was a miniature version of the one that powered the Royal train that conveyed King George VI and Queen Elizabeth on part of their cross Canada trip in 1939.

Miniature steam locomotive 6400, which operated during the Christmas season from 1945 until 1962, frequently carried as many as 4 000 happy children a day around its Eaton's Toyland route.

For my younger two brothers and I a trip to Toyland was preceded by a visit to Eaton's Beddings and Linens on the second floor where stacks of winter clothing — snow suits, extra woollen socks, soggy mittens, rubber boots, peaked hats with ear flaps, and so on, would be left in the care of my Aunt Peggy, who worked in the department, while Mom took us upstairs to visit Santa. The windows where Aunt Peg worked looked out onto a busy, often snow-covered Yonge Street. Santa would have to wait while I watched the packed Peter Witt streetcars with their equally packed trailers rumble by. (The subway was still a few years in the future.) And while those streetcars were fun to watch, the lure of Toyland, and two impatient brothers, always won out.

In those far-off days Eaton's and Simpson's had only one Toronto store each (malls and shopping centres were years in the future), and just as families back then were readers of either the *Telegram* or *Star* newspaper, so too families were disciples (oops, perhaps a bad choice of words considering the season) of either Eaton's or Simpson's. As it happened the Fileys were a *Tely* and Eaton's family. Why? Who knows.

Now that I think back on it, perhaps it was because of the "Santagrams" that appeared in the *Telegram* every night for weeks, plus the unequalled merriment of all those floats in the annual Eaton sponsored Santa Claus Parade. Back then it was just a lot of fun. Now I realize it was all a marketing ploy. Ah, gee!

EVOLUTION OF A "MEETING PLACE"

December 28, 1997

N ext Thursday, January 1, 1998, the evolution of our city will continue as the communities of Etobicoke, North York, York, Scarborough, and East York join with Toronto to create a new City of Toronto.

This evolution of our city began in 1793 with the establishment of a small community on the north shore of Lake Ontario in the recently created Province of Upper Canada. The site selected by John Graves Simcoe, the first lieutenant governor, had originally been used by the Native people as a place to meet and discuss matters of importance. In their language, it was a *toronto*, a meeting place.

THE MUNICIPALITY OF METROPOLITAN TORONTO
24-INCH WATER MAIN
PROJECT Nº I

SLIE B. ALLAN
SSIONER OF WORKS.

FREDERICK G. GARDINER
CHAIRMAN.

Metro's Works Commissioner Leslie Allan, its Chairman Fred Gardiner, and Toronto Mayor Leslie Saunders at the official opening of Metro's project #1, August 9, 1954.

They were followed in the early 1700s by French explorers who chose a site on the nearby Humber River as the location of the first of several small fur-trading outposts. One of the subsequent forts was built near today's band shell on the CNE grounds. The French occupation of the area ended in 1759, and soon Toronto came under British influence. But another 34 years would pass before the site of the future City of Toronto would again see settlers.

In 1793 Simcoe, who feared an invasion by American forces intent on resuming hostilities against her English foe, selected Toronto because of one of its physical characteristics, an easily defensible harbour. He believed the harbour was the perfect place for the building of ships to protect his new province from the anticipated invasion. While the harbour is now accessible via two entrances, back then only a single entrance at the west end existed, which was easily protected by defence works in the form of a blockhouse and cannon on the peninsula (now Toronto Island) and a pallisaded garrison (now called Fort York) on the mainland. Or so Simcoe believed. In fact, Simcoe's worst fear was to be realized in the spring of 1813, but that's another story for another time.

With shipbuilding came the need for accommodation for the workers and their families. Houses were built, streets laid out, and the seeds of our present-day Toronto were sown. At first, the little community continued to be called Toronto, a name that was described as being "foreign to the governor's ear." As a result, Simcoe quickly changed that name to the more "regal sounding" York to honour the son of the reigning King George III, Frederick, the Duke of York.

As the town grew, not only in population but in commerce and wealth statistics, as well, so too did the need to provide the mundane but nevertheless essential civic amenities such as sewers and sidewalks. In legalese, it became necessary to provide a more efficient system of police and municipal government, and to do so a royal decree was passed on March 6, 1834, elevating the little town of York, population 9 254, to the status of city. To avoid possible confusion with a place in the States called New York, the community's original name was reinstated. The City of Toronto was born.

As the city grew over the succeeding years, so too did the small communities surrounding it. By 1883, the Town of Yorkville, Toronto's "bedroom suburb," was suffering from the same problems that had plagued the Town of York years earlier, the inability to provide the necessary public amenities. Annexation was the only answer. Other fast-growing communities surrounding the city, Riverdale, Parkdale, Rosedale, North Toronto, and so on, eventually began to suffer the same problems. They too were annexed by Toronto with the last major annexation, that of the Town of North Toronto, occurring in 1912. With that addition the city had grown nearly 400% since its creation in 1834 and had a population well in excess of 200 000.

The city's boundaries remained virtually unchanged over the next few decades while the population of the outlying townships,

Etobicoke, Scarborough, and York, grew dramatically. It was from the former that Long Branch, Mimico, and New Toronto were carved with the townships of North York and East York and the villages of Leaside, Weston, Forest Hill, and Swansea severed from the latter.

With the large influx of new Canadians into the city, villages and townships following the end of the Second World War, it quickly became obvious that some sort of overriding authority would have to be created to look after numerous inter-community problems such as the building of new roads, water mains, and sewage treatment facilities, improved policing, construction of affordable housing, and so on, each of which had become a serious impediment. That new authority was the Municipality of Metropolitan Toronto, which went into business on February 15, 1953.

Because the citizens of North York were constantly short of water, the new corporation's first project was the laying of a new 24-inch water main from the city's huge Roselawn water tank via Roselawn Avenue, Caldow Road, and Hillhurst Boulevard to Bathurst Street, where it connected with the North York supply system. Water began flowing in the line on August 9, 1954.

Now, with Metro's work done and, most will agree, done well, it's only natural that Toronto continue to evolve into one great city without the impediments spawned by artificial borders.

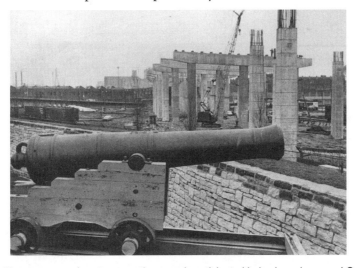

Now a source of controversy, the eagerly anticipated Lakeshore (renamed Gardiner) Expressway was another of Metro's pioneer projects. Original plans had it soaring over part of historic Fort York. Fortunately, saner heads prevailed, and the route was altered away from the fort.

THE MORE THINGS CHANGE...

January 4, 1998

The editorial in the local newspaper seemed to say it all:"It is a gloomy moment in history. Not for many years now — not in the lifetime of most readers of this newspaper — has there been so much grave and deep apprehension; never has the future seemed so incalculable as at this time."

Now before you think I'm about to start the new year with a column full of gloom and doom, let me point out that the above statement doesn't refer to such modern-day concerns as Iraq's defiant posturing or Asia's economic difficulties or even Quebec's possible separation from the rest of the country. In fact, the words were penned exactly 50 years ago by the editor of the old Toronto *Evening Telegram*. However, I've used this old newspaper quote simply to demonstrate that even though we think things are going badly today, it's all happened before. Perhaps not the exact same problems, but problems nevertheless.

In 1948, the year the *Telegram* editorial was published, communities along Weston Road were served by streetcars like the one seen in this view looking north at Dundas and Keele streets. However, before 1948 came to an end the Weston Road streetcar would be no more.

Let me prove my point by taking a quick trip back in time to see what was upsetting people in Toronto as the new year of 1948 dawned. First, the festive season wasn't as colourful as in past years with government restrictions on Christmas lighting in force. The directive read, "All outside decorative lighting, including Christmas trees, is prohibited." Those grinches! Actually the government had to do it owing to a severe shortage of electrical generating facilities throughout the province. That same problem would lead to the end of the Weston Road, North Yonge, and Spadina streetcars later that year.

In Etobicoke Township, outside workers were agitated that even though the minimum hourly wage had been increased to 86¢, they were still faced with a 44-hour week. Up in Ottawa, the federal government was concerned with whether the CBC could afford to get involved with the latest communications marvel, television. One engineer estimated that to set up just one station could cost the government the enormous sum of $250,000! (CBC, in the form of CBLT, Toronto's first TV station, finally went on the air on September 8, 1952.) And would food prices ever level off? In early 1948 Grade A turkeys had risen to 59¢ a pound, porterhouse steak was 49¢ while the same amount of bacon, sliced, was 57¢. Oranges were 48¢ a dozen, apples 5 for a quarter. Bread was a dime a loaf, eggs 55¢ a dozen, and a chocolate bar 7¢. Hand soap was 11¢ a bar, a pair of women's furred overshoes sold for $4.95 and, if you had the money, a 5-tube cabinet radio, complete with phonograph, was a whopping $439. Where will it all end?

Here in Toronto drivers were steaming over an unwanted New Year's gift. Gasoline prices had increased again, and a gallon of the "No. 1 grade" had soared to 39¢. Customs officers at nearby border crossings were issued yardsticks to help catch drivers smuggling gasoline back from the States. And as if that increase wasn't enough the Ontario government raised the price of a man's haircut to 50¢ from 45¢ with 15¢ head rubs and 20¢ shaves increased proportionately.

But here's problem we all wish we still faced. Fifty years ago fans were wondering if the Leafs could maintain their first-place position over the other five teams in the NHL. They did, and you'd be showing your age if you say you remember the team winning the Stanley Cup that season. In fact, you'd be showing your age if you can remember the Leafs ever winning the Cup.

Oh, well, a Happy New Year, anyway!

THE TRAGIC TRUTH

January 11, 1998

I t would be wrong to say that the media coverage given the recent release of James Cameron's epic film *Titanic* approached the coverage given the disaster that befell the ship back in April, 1912. It only seems that way.

In fact, had the first reports that appeared in the newspapers worldwide on Monday, April 15, 1912, reporting on the giant liner's collision with an iceberg in the North Atlantic some 400 miles off Cape Race, Newfoundland, been anywhere near correct, there's no doubt that there wouldn't have been a film at all.

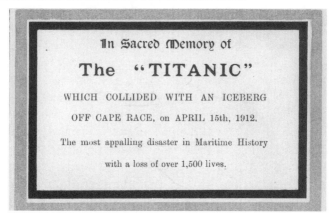

In Sacred Memory of

The "TITANIC"

WHICH COLLIDED WITH AN ICEBERG

OFF CAPE RACE, on APRIL 15th, 1912.

The most appalling disaster in Maritime History

with a loss of over 1,500 lives.

I found this melancholy memorial card while rummaging through a second-hand book store several years ago. On one side was a view of *Titanic* with the wording reproduced here on the other.

The story made Toronto's various daily newspapers, the *Evening Telegram*, *Star*, *Globe* and *Mail and Empire*, but only in a minor way. In the case of the *Telegram* the story was found inside on page 13 under the headline, "Passengers Safe, Leaving *Titanic*, Two Liners Assisting In Rescue".

The report continued, "The latest messages from the crippled steamship indicate safety of all passengers with the steamers *Carpathia* and *Parisian* early on the scene and others standing by." According to these first reports, between 800 and 1 200 of *Titanic*'s complement of passengers and crew had already been transferred to

Carpathia. While this must have come as welcome news for family and friends on board *Titanic*, the truth was that when *Carpathia*, outbound for the Mediterranean from New York City (coincidentally the latter port was *Titanic*'s intended destination), heard the call for help she was 58 miles distant from the collision site. Even steaming as fast as she could, the 10-year-old Canard liner didn't arrive until early the next morning, Tuesday, April 16, more than an hour after *Titanic* began its plunge to the bottom. Nevertheless, *Carpathia* was the first to arrive and rescued 705 of the 2 228 on board Titanic. Sadly, and in spite of those early news reports, 1 523 souls wouldn't be so fortunate.

A postcard view of the rescue ship *Carpathia*.

Today, in an age of lightning fast communications, it's difficult to understand how officials could permit such an inaccurate report to be printed. But we have the 20/20 vision afforded by hindsight. Back then, there were no satellites in space with telescopes surveying the world situation, no U-2 flights, no helicopters hovering over the action. There was no radio (that was a decade in the future), no television (exactly 40 years would pass before Toronto would get its first local TV station) and, as hard as it may be for younger readers to fathom (get it?), even the now ubiquitous CNN was still many decades in the future (the Cable News Network went on the air June 1, 1980).

In 1912, the world, including the people in the various newsrooms in the farthest corners of the globe, had to rely on Guglielmo Marconi's turn-of-the-century invention, wireless telegraphy, for reports of fast-breaking news. And so it was as the bits and pieces (as opposed to today's bits and bytes) came available they were quickly, and not always accurately, turned into stories for the newspapers' eager readers.

So inaccurate were the incoming telegraph reports that at one point, they even had the stricken liner making her way, slowly and under her own power, to the Port of Halifax. Then an updated report had the ship under tow. As a result of these two reports people awaiting the arrival of some of the wealthier personages on board *Titanic* rerouted their private trains from the original New York City destination to Halifax in order that the travellers not be inconvenienced further.

Unfortunately, all these early reports gave was false hope, and by the time the Toronto papers hit the streets the following day the true story of the disaster was clear. The mighty and, as many believed, the unsinkable *Titanic* had gone to the bottom.

One of the 705 survivors rescued by the Cunard liner *Carpathia* was Major Arthur Peuchen, a Torontonian who soon after his arrival in Toronto began to feel the adverse effects of what had at first been regarded as his good fortune. More about the major in next week's column as well as the story about the man who was directly responsible for *Titanic*'s creation, a man who was born right here in Canada.

Readers who wish to learn more about *Titanic* are invited to join The Titanic Historical Society, P.O. Box 51053, Indian Orchard, Massachusetts, USA 01151-0053.

MORE TALES OF THE TITANIC

January 18, 1998

Even though more than 85 years have passed since what many said couldn't happen did happen, fascinating stories about the ill-fated *Titanic* continue to unfold.

Two of the those stories have direct connections with our country. One concerns the man who was directly responsible for the design and construction of the great ship, a man who was born right here in Canada. The other deals with a Torontonian whose actions on board *Titanic* that cold Sunday night would have given him hero status in today's society. But in 1912, he was judged differently, something that was to haunt him for the rest of his life.

William James Pirrie (1847–1924), *Titanic*'s father.

William James Pirrie, the son of recently arrived Irish immigrant parents, was born in Quebec City on May 31, 1847. For reasons not known, Pirrie's stay in the province of his birth was short, the family returning to Belfast before the youngster had turned three.

At the age of 15 Pirrie was apprenticed to a local shipbuilding firm owned by Edward Harland and Gustav Wolff, where he learned on the job and quickly rose through the ranks. In 1869, when still just 22, Pirrie was appointed chief draughtsman on a project to build the steamship *Oceanic*, a vessel that was to become the newly established White Star Line's first ship.

Thirty-eight years later officials of the White Star Line, which had developed into a highly successful shipping concern, met with Pirrie, now chairman of the Harland and Wolff organization, to discuss the building of a trio of giant new ocean liners for White Star's Atlantic service. The first and third would be known, respectively, as *Olympic* and *Britannic*. The other, at first simply referred to as hull #401, would be launched on May 31, 1911, and given the name *Titanic*.

In recognition of his service to Britain and its shipbuilding industry, Pirrie was created a baron in 1906 and a viscount in 1921. Lord Pirrie was 77 when he died, on board ship, on June 6, 1924.

Another Canadian closely connect with *Titanic* was Arthur Godfrey Peuchen, a Toronto businessman who was both a passenger on *Titanic* and a survivor. This latter fact would cause Peuchen great distress on his return to Toronto.

Peuchen was born in Montreal in 1859. When he was 12, the Peuchen family moved to Toronto, but not much more is known about the young Peuchen until he appears in the city directories of the early 1880s as owner of a paint and varnish business located first at 10 Church Street and then in a factory at Leslie Street and Eastern Avenue.

We do know that in 1897, with the assistance of ubiquitous Sir William Mackenzie, Peuchen established the Standard Chemical Company, the main product of which was acetone recovered from

Arthur Godfrey Peuchen (1859–1929), *Titanic* hero.

the distillation of wood. At that time acetone was a key ingredient in the manufacture of ammunition, and it was to return from a sales trip to England and the continent promoting the company's product to countries not unaccustomed to warring amongst themselves that Peuchen book first-class passage on the maiden voyage of *Titanic*.

For Peuchen the crossing was a series of social events and he was very much at home dining and chatting with many of the other 329 first-class passengers. At exactly 11:40 p.m. on Sunday, April 14, Peuchen, in his stateroom, C104, preparing for bed, felt the mighty *Titanic* shudder and minutes later noticed that the ship's huge engines had stopped. Sensing something was amiss, he ventured out on deck, but not before dressing warmly. Assuming he'd soon return to the cabin Peuchen left securities valued at more than $300 000 in a tin box on the dresser.

Once on deck, he made his way to the lifeboats where passengers were milling around not exactly sure what to do next. Peuchen soon found himself in the vicinity of lifeboat #6 just as it was being filled. Suddenly someone shouted that there was only one crew member in the boat. Second Officer Lightoller cried out that a second experienced person was needed. Peuchen stepped forward and offered his services, announcing that while not a seaman he was an experienced yachtsman. (Peuchen was a member of Toronto's Royal Canadian Yacht Club.) Lightoller then ordered Peuchen into the lifeboat, and it was lowered.

Once on board the rescue ship Peuchen, perhaps anticipating that his own survival would be, to say the least, controversial, especially once it became known how many women and children had perished, requested a note signed by the Second Officer confirming that Peuchen had, in fact, been ordered into the boat. He also asked many of the women in his lifeboat to sign the back of a menu attesting to the fact that Peuchen had helped them in their time of need.

Once home, Peuchen's documents were ignored, and he soon found himself ostracized by friends and public alike. Finally, unable to withstand the constant criticism of his actions, he retired from the Queen's Own Rifles and from business life and in 1915 moved to western Canada. He took ill in the fall of 1929, returned to Toronto, and died at his residence at 105 Roxborough Street East on December 9 of that year.

Peuchen was never forgiven.

A SPIN DOWN AUTO ROW

January 25, 1998

In an earlier life I was a chemical technologist working with the Ontario Water Resources Commission, a government agency that would eventually become part of the Ministry of the Environment. When I started with the OWRC back in 1965 the first office desk, chair, and coat rack I ever had was located in a building at 801 Bay Street, just north of the old Eaton's College Street store.

The new McLaughlin Building, Bay Street north of College, 1925.

Recently, while visiting Jack Webster at the Police Museum near Bay and College, I decided to take a tour of my old stomping grounds. And what did I find? Not only has someone levelled my old office, they've knocked down the whole bloomin' building. Walking north on Bay Street I was amazed at the transformation of the street that has taken place since I left the Commission. I can remember wandering up to Bay and Wellesley to see the latest cars in the Ontario Automobile and O'Donnell-Morrison automobile showrooms. Now it's a street of condominiums. However, one of those showrooms survives still, that of Addison on Bay at the northwest corner of Bay and Grenville streets. Here a selection of shiny new Cadillac, Pontiac, and Buick models sit all nice and cosy, and free of those darn salt stains, behind large picture windows.

When the building opened back in May of 1925, that same showroom was packed with a handsome array of McLaughlin-Buicks. That was only natural since the place was the McLaughlin Building. I'll bet that title, which was carved into the stonework over the main entrance, still exists under the modern Addison sign. The building was put up by General Motors Corporation Company of Canada (as GM was known in the newspapers of the day) exactly seven years after the American parent company completed a deal begun in 1914 that gave it total control of the long-time McLaughlin Motor Car Company in Oshawa.

The first McLaughlin automobile rolled out of the Oshawa factory in December, 1907. The car was powered by a two-cylinder engine and contained a number of other parts purchased from the Buick Car Company in Flint, Michigan, and it wasn't long before people were referring to the Oshawa built vehicles as McLaughlin-Buicks. At first that name distressed the ultra patriotic Sam McLaughlin. However by 1923 the hyphenated name had become standard as the Oshawa built product became more and more like the American Buick. The once-proud McLaughlin name vanished altogether when car production was turned over to the war effort following introduction of the 1942 models.

Same building, still a GM car dealership, as it appears today.

The McLaughlin Building on Bay Street was just the first of many new auto showrooms that would be erected on either side of the street in the years following 1925. On view were products such as Whippets, Stearns-Knights, and Willys-Knights from the Weston Road factory of Willys-Overland, De Sotos at National Motors, and Dodge cars at Moore and Hughes. Reo Motor Sales featured Reo and Wolverine cars, Bay Motors had Marmons, while nearby Auburn

Motor Sales had the awesome Auburn, and Breay-Nash Motors was offering the Nash line of cars. As an added touch, just off Bay Street on Breadalbane, Packard Motors Ltd. were showing their magnificent vehicles.

No wonder the stretch of Bay between College and Bloor was dubbed Auto Row. To emphasize that fact, the building at the southeast corner of Bloor and Bay was the scene of the most popular car unveiling in the city's history, for it was there, in 1928, that Torontonians met the exciting new Ford Model A.

MEASURE OF SUCCESS

February 8, 1998

As Toronto becomes larger and more sophisticated we frequently tend to forget the things that happened along the way that helped propel us into that assembly of what are known collectively as (and boy do I hate this term) "world-class cities."

Take for instance the appearance on the skyline of Toronto's first real skyscraper. To be sure throughout its history the city has had all kinds of tall buildings, the Temple Building at Bay and Richmond (10 storeys, 1895, demolished), the Trader's Bank at Yonge and Colborne (15 storeys, 1905), and the Royal Bank at King and Yonge (20 storeys, 1913 to 1915), to name just a few. But for the citizens and visitors to Toronto 60 or so years ago the building that really turned heads skyward was the Bank of Commerce Building on King Street West at Jordan (now described as Commerce Court North).

The weather beacon on top of Canada Life's University Avenue head office flashed on for the first time nearly 47 years ago. This photo shows the street in the late 1950s, when it was still relatively free of office towers.

Work on the new head office for the bank started just about the same time that the financial picture worldwide was beginning to turn sour, very sour indeed as we all now know. Nevertheless, work went ahead and even as the world slipped into a depression the new massive bank building continued to take shape. The months went by, and the world slipped further and further into a state of hopelessness. Then, at exactly 10:30 on the morning of April 2, 1930, a hint of good times ahead (far ahead, as history now tells us) rang out 434 feet above King Street when the gang of steelworkers in the employ of the Hamilton Bridge Company gave a cheer as the final section of steel was bolted into place. Toronto's Bank of Commerce was the tallest structure not just in the country, but in the entire British Empire.

Over the next few months the tenants (to be precise 2 500 of them) moved into their offices on the 10th to 31st floors of the 34-storey structure. It wasn't until February 2, 1931, that the bank, whose 700 employees occupied the 4 underground floors as well as the first 9 floors above street level, was officially opened to the general public.

On August 9, 1951, Torontonians looked to the top of another building, one that had also been completed in 1931. This time, however, they gazed skyward for a totally different reason. It was on that day that the new weather beacon on top of the University Avenue head office of the Canada Life Assurance Company flashed on for the first time. For nearly 47 years that 41-foot-high beacon, consisting of 1 007 40-watt bulbs and located 351 feet above street level, has prognosticated the next day's weather using neon tubes, green for clear, steady red for cloudy, flashing red for rain, and flashing white for snow. The tower lights remain steady when no temperature change is expected, appear to climb if rising temperatures are in the future or descending of it's going to be colder.

Both steel and masonry work on the city's first real skyscraper, the 34-storey Bank of Commerce Building on King Street west of Yonge, are almost complete in this 1930 photo.

TORONTO AUTO SHOWS HAVE ALWAYS BEEN POPULAR

February 15, 1998

One of the few bright and shiny things about this dark and dismal time of year is the Canadian International Auto Show. The event opened last Friday and will run through to next Sunday, February 22. This year there's a slight change in the venue with the entire show, all half a million square feet of it, being staged in its entirety in the recently enlarged Metro Toronto Convention Centre on the south side of Front Street just west of Union Station.

Projected attendance figures for this year's show predict that some 230 000 people will come, ogle, and dream. That number is a far cry from the 80 000 who turned up for first edition of the show, an event

Not long after those first car shows at the Granite Club and the Armouries, displays of new cars became a popular attraction at the annual Canadian National Exhibition. In this photo the then three-year-old Automotive Building was hosting a huge variety of 1932 models. The last new-car show to be held at the CNE was in 1967. The show is now held each February in the mammoth Toronto Convention Centre.

that started off with the somewhat parochial title of Toronto International Auto Show. It was held in mid-February way back in 1974 at the Toronto International Centre of Commerce out by the airport. My high school math skills reveal that this year's event will be the 25th auto show (remember 1974 is number one, 1975, number two, and so on. Sorry to harp on it, but I still remember trying to convince the post office that the 1978 CNE was the 100th fair with the first one held in 1879. They never did get it and put the wrong dates, 1878–1978, on the Ex's commemorative stamp.)

The American-built Northern first appeared in 1902 and is seen in postal service here at the Exhibition.

As exciting as each year's shows have become, the actual holding of such a show is certainly nothing new here in Toronto. At first these "shows" were shows in name only as each of the city's pioneer dealers simply put a selection of his vehicles on display in his own showroom and invited prospective buyers to stop by. It wasn't until 1906 that dealers, manufacturers, and importers of European machines got together and presented the first all-inclusive shows. In that year there were two competing shows, one at the old Granite Club rink on Church Street, the other in the sprawling Armouries on University Avenue, where the Court House now stands.

The idea of displaying the latest in horseless-carriage technology may have been introduced to Torontonians in 1906, but the desire to examine or better still own one of the newfangled machines had been around for years. And as new as electric cars may seem to us today, the very first car to kick up dust (and other things) on Toronto's horse-and-buggy saturated thoroughfares was an electric. Toronto's pioneer motorist was the well-known patent attorney Frederick Barnard Fetherstonaugh who, tapping the talents of inventor and client William Still, became the proud owner of our city's first automobile. It was powered using a small electric motor connected to a storage battery. Unlike modern-day electric car owners, back in 1893 Fetherstonaugh didn't have to take his car to a special "filling" station where the car is plugged in and left to recharge. No sir, Fred simply ran a power line from his garage out to the radial streetcar overhead just outside his place on the old Lake Shore Road near Church Street (now Royal York Road). Using a simple step-down transformer and a few other electrical thingamabobs, the crafty motorist had a freshly recharged motor ready to whisk him to his office in the old Bank of Commerce at 25 King Street West each morning. He probably parked right in front of the building, like some drivers still do.

BAYVIEW GHOSTS STILL HAUNT TORONTO

February 22, 1998

An aerial view of the Bayview Ghost as it looked in 1965, with the Bayview Extension in the background.

Whenever the subject turns to memories of buildings Toronto has lost over the years, one that's frequently mentioned is the famous, or should I say infamous, Bayview Ghost.

While the loss of some of our buildings evokes anger, in the case of this structure its eventual demolition was a happy turn of events for just about everyone.

For those who are new to our city, or for those who are too young to remember, the ghost was an incomplete white brick shell of a building that stood on the west side of the Bayview Extension, just south of Nesbitt Drive. The original plan put forward by the proponents of this project, the Canadian Construction Company, would have seen the 7-storey building in the photo, along with a quartet of 20-storey buildings, erected on a prime piece of Borough of East York property overlooking the Don Valley.

These five buildings, to be known collectively as Hampton Park, would have a grand total of 913 suites. Construction work began in the summer of 1959 even though the nearby residents were vigorously voicing their concerns to whoever would listen.

A building permit was issued authorizing the construction of two of the buildings. Then, to use a construction phrase no contractor ever wants to hear, the roof fell in. Various government bodies began to object, some because of the project's location in what was to be part of the Don Valley green belt area. Borough officials were concerned because of the lack of sewers and water mains to service the project. With those buildings surrounded by ravines the cost of installing the mains and sewers would be astronomical.

There was also the problem of automobile access to and from the site. Metro didn't want all those vehicles dumped onto the newly built Bayview Extension, and the nearby residents certainly didn't want them on the side streets.

Over the next few years plans continued to surface. One idea would have seen the original plan changed drastically, with the partially built structure the only building. Another idea would have the Bayview Ghost, a name with which the East York council

The remarkable True Davidson (1901–1978).

members were not amused, exorcised and a complex of town houses built. Joining in on the fun, a Toronto *Sun* editorial on October 5, 1973, declared that the eyesore should be retained for historic reasons and promoted as Metro's Stonehenge. Nothing happened.

In 1975, another developer purchased the eyesore with a plan to demolish it and erect a town house complex on the site. But until that plan was approved, the developer was ordered by East York officials to secure the site or demolish the shell. Again, nothing happened.

More years went by, and in 1981 another town house project surfaced, this time featuring 440 units. In time the idea was approved by the Ontario Municipal Board, only to be revoked by the provincial cabinet.

Finally, on October 30, 1981, more than 22 years after work started on the ill-fated structure (and fittingly the day before Halloween) the wrecker's ball began to swing, and in hours the Bayview Ghost was no more. There's little doubt the site will be developed, but to what extent no one knows.

To learn more about this strange story, as well as the fascinating life story of a person deeply involved with all facets of East York's development, pick up a copy of Eleanor Dark's book *Call Me True*. True Davidson moved to East York in 1947, served first as a school trustee and was elected to East York council in 1958. She served as mayor from 1967 to 1969. A fascinating book about a fascinating lady.

LIVING HIGH OFF HOGTOWN'S PAST

March 1, 1998

A t the extreme east end of Front Street East, where it turns
north and connects with the south end of the Bayview
Extension, are the remains of a large, hulking building that is
slowly but surely being torn apart by a demolition company. Before
long it will be no more. To anyone driving or cycling by (it's unlikely
there'll be an pedestrians in the area) at first glance the old structure
appears to be just another of those ancient factories no longer in use.
Therefore, down it comes. In fact, for most people its disappearance
will go unnoticed or unheralded.

Over the years the William Davies Front Street plant was expanded and modernized.
In this February, 1998, view wreckers begin their task of tearing apart.

But as with a number of the old buildings scattered around town,
this place, or rather what's left of this place, has an interesting
connection with our city's past. To be more precise, with a term that
was, and in some quarters still is used to describe Toronto...Hogtown!

To be completely accurate it can be argued that the term *hogtown*
may have more than one origin. For instance, some suggest that it
comes from one of the first laws on the new city's books, the one that
prohibited hogs running at large. Here is that law, identified as Bylaw
#474, passed by the City Council in October of 1868.

That it shall not be lawful for any person or persons to suffer his, her or their entire horse, bull, goat or swine to run at large within the limits of the said city.

Any animal subsequently caught was impounded, and in the case of swine, a fine of 10¢ per hog per day was imposed. Exactly why hogs were centred out as being descriptive of Toronto and why they were described as *entire* as opposed to *partial* — a partial swine? — is unknown. Why not Horsetown, or Bulltown or even Goattown? Don't know.

A more likely suggestion for the origin of the word "hogtown" perhaps has to do with the old building being demolished on Front Street. In its heyday more hogs were slaughtered and processed in this plant than in any other in the country. In fact, it is reported that in the latter years of the nineteenth century more hogs were processed in the Front Street building than anywhere else on the continent save for Chicago. As a result, for Canadians at least, Toronto was *the* hog town.

Hogtown pioneer
William Davies (1831–1921).

To take this assumption a step further, we could also say that William Davies was the person responsible for the term *hogtown*, since he was the owner of the company that did all that hog processing. Davies was born in England in 1831 and emigrated to Canada when he was just 24 years of age. His original intention was to be a farmer, but he quickly decided he'd be better off using the experience he had gained in the provisions business in the old country.

Davies rented a shop in the St. Lawrence market, purchased various cuts of pork from slaughterhouses in and around the city, and began selling hams and bacon cured using a procedure he had developed. By 1861 his meat products were in such demand that he found it necessary to build a larger processing plant. His new place at the southwest corner of Front (then called Palace) and Frederick streets was the first such facility in the entire country (which was still a few years away from confederation) devoted exclusively to the curing of pork products. Incidentally, a portion of this building still stands, though now converted to less messy office-type uses.

Back in the 1860s refrigeration techniques had not yet been developed, meaning that this plant could only operate in the fall or winter months. To fulfil the ever-increasing number of orders (Great Britain was an especially good market for him), Davies shipped millions of pounds of pork products packed in brine. Thus the term *meat packers*.

In 1874 the volume of orders once again necessitated increased space. A new plant, incorporating both slaughtering and processing operations, was opened on Front Street near the Don River. Twenty-three years later artificial refrigeration equipment was installed, again a first for Canada. The Front Street plant grew like Topsy, and soon a variety of buildings occupied the site. A more modern processing plant opened on St. Clair Avenue west of Keele Street in 1903, and operations at the old Front Street location were eventually phased out. In 1927, the William Davies Company became part of Canada Packers.

Sketch of William Davies Company's Front Street hog processing plant soon after it opened in 1874.

MEET THE KNIGHT WHO BUILT OUR CASTLE

March 8, 1998

It was on this day 59 years ago that one of Canada's most influential and successful businessmen passed away. Sadly, in his twilight years this unfortunate Torontonian would not hear such accolades, but rather words of derision, which hurt him deeply. In fact, it wasn't until the news of Sir Henry Pellatt's death became known that the public gave recognition to the fact that the elderly knight, who had built Toronto's castle on the hill, had performed a great deal of good during his lifetime.

Henry Mill Pellatt was born in Kingston, Ontario, in 1859. Two years later the Pellatt family moved to Toronto, where the father eventually entered into a partnership with a young Edmund Osler and established the brokerage firm of Pellatt and Osler. In 1876, the young Pellatt joined the firm as a clerk. Seven years later, when Osler decided to go it on his own, Pellatt moved up the corporate ladder eventually becoming a full partner in a firm referred to as Pellatt and Pellatt.

Henry's business insight was brilliant, and when he heard of the successes American inventor Thomas Edison was having with artificial lighting, he quickly established the Toronto Electric Light Company. He obtained a contract from the city and installed a total of 32 electric arc lights on downtown streets. He was making money, and before long a great deal of it. He continued to invest in businesses that took advantage of themiracle of the age, that mysterious power source of power that illuminated streets and magically moved heavy street railway cars, something called electricity. So he put his money into the Toronto Railway Company, the city's privately owned transit operator that by 1894 would be totally reliant on electricity power their hundreds of streetcars.

And to supply that power he invested in the new Electrical Development Company of Ontario, which would soon speed electricity into the city from a huge generating plant at Niagara Falls. Henry also invested in land in western Canada, and in the newly established Canadian Pacific Railway. He reasoned that an influx of European immigrants would willingly pay good money for the land as well as more money for railway tickets to get them there.

Sir Henry Pellatt views a painting of himself as a young man during a dinner given in his honour at Casa Loma shortly before his death in 1939.

One of his foreign investments was in a fledgling company we know today as Brascan.

Henry was a keen monarchist and deeply interested in the pomp and circumstance associated with the military. These two passions saw Henry pay $150 000 out of his pocket to take 640 members of his beloved Queen's Own Rifles to the 1910 war games in England. Concerned that his King and Queen wouldn't have an appropriate place to stay if they visited Toronto, he undertook to spend several million dollars to build Casa Loma. If they did come to town, boy, would they have a place to stay. These overly extravagant expenditures plus the firm's somewhat shady dealings with the Home Bank, which collapsed in 1923 and caused great hardship for many of its middle- and low-income clients, led to a rejection of the man and a general distrust of his motives.

Behind his back some even called him a buffoon.

Business setbacks and the onslaught of the Great Depression caused the bubble to finally burst. Sir Henry died a sad and penniless man.

It wasn't until his death on this day in 1939 that people began to reflect on the momentous things Sir Henry had done during his lifetime. His funeral cortege from St. James' Cathedral to the Forest Lawn Mausoleum on north Yonge Street drew the largest crowd of mourners in the city's history.

Virtually penniless in his latter years Pellatt, the man who built Casa Loma, died in the back room of a small suburban house. It was owned by his former chauffeur, one of his few real friends.

SPORTMEN'S SHOW TURNS 50

March 15, 1998

The old YMCA building on College Street (now the site of Toronto Police Service Headquarters) was where the idea of a Sportsmen's Show was first discussed.

This year marks the 50th anniversary of the popular Sportsmen's Show. The very first Sportsmen's Show, known as Canadian National Sportsmen's Show, started on exactly the same day as it does this year, March 13, 1948. The event was the brainchild of Frank Kortright, a prominent businessman who would soon become general manager of the internationally known A. R. Clarke Leather Co. on Toronto's Eastern Avenue and who had assumed the presidency of the Toronto Anglers' and Hunters' Association in 1946.

This association had been established as the Toronto Anglers' Association (the Hunters' part wasn't added until the mid-1930s) on the night of March 27, 1925, when a group of 25 local sportsmen got together in the old YMCA building on College Street (where the Toronto Police Headquarters is now located). The focus of the new organization was to encourage the conservation of Ontario's wildlife in its many forms. Tourism into the province was just beginning to grow, and it was felt that without proper foresight and management the very reasons people were eager to visit Ontario would soon be wiped out by exploitation of its wildlife resources.

Ardent sportsman and well-known writer Greg Clark (left) chats with Sportsmen's Show founder Frank Kortright.

Not long after Frank Kortright had assumed office, he was able to convince the association membership that what was really needed was an event that, through the use of entertainment and education, would arouse the general public's interest in the great out-of-doors. Kortright was sure that visitors to this event, whatever it was to be called, would quickly see the value and long-term benefits that would result from conservation of the province's fields, forests, and streams.

In order not to put the association into financial disarray should the fledgling event turn out to be a failure, Kortright solicited the help of several prominent businesspeople to underwrite $60 000 of the $90 000 that the first event, which had been given the name Sportsmen's Show, would cost to stage. Some of those benefactors were in the forefront of Ontario's business community of half a century ago, most with names that many long-time Torontonians will still recall — R.A. Laidlaw of the Laidlaw Lumber Company, L. M. Savage of the Savage Shoe Company, K. M. Kilbourn of Wickett and Craig, Limited, and Aubrey Davis of the Davis Leather Company in Newmarket, Ontario (coincidentally the Davis of Davis Drive). So respected was Kortright that a couple of these benefactors were actually his competitors in the leather and tanning business. An interesting sidelight to the birth of this show has to do with Elwood Hughes, the general manager of the

CNE back then. Some of the promoters thought that one way to get a better deal on the Coliseum, in which they wanted to stage the show, was to get Hughes to visit a similar show in the States. Surely the success of the American versions would go a long way to encouraging the Ex to lower its rental fee. Unfortunately, one of the cities on the trip itinerary was Memphis where the entourage was met with a freezing rainstorm. No sooner had Hughes stepped out of the car to enter the show building than he slipped and fell, breaking his arm in the process. Any further twisting of that arm was obviously out of the question.

Nevertheless, the Toronto show went on. Was it a success? Without question, yes, with more than $15 000 in profits turned over to assist in the funding of various conservation efforts of the day.

Just in case you thought you'd heard or read that name Kortright somewhere before, he's the name behind the Kortright Centre, a project established in 1973 as a result of a $150 000 donation by the Sportsmen's Shows to the Metro Toronto and Region Conservation Association in honour of this concerned Canadian who had passed away the previous year.

Since that first Sportsmen's Show held in Toronto exactly 50 years ago this week, some $26 million has been committed to ongoing conservation programs.

**A reader writes that in the early 1920s residents of Central Street in west Toronto asked city council to change the name of their street to Wanda Avenue. Why Wanda? he asks. Anyone out there know?

I received several replies as to just who Wanda might have been. Two of the most interesting came from readers in Kingston and Don Mills. Both suggested that the Wanda referred to in the street name may have been Wanda Hawley, an extremely popular silent screen movie actress during the era under question. Wanda Hawley was born in Pennsylvania in 1897 and appeared in some 50 films between 1917 and 1927; she was usually cast in the role of a vampy seductress. Wanda also appeared in several big-budget Cecil B. DeMille productions, and for a time rivalled Paramount's Gloria Swanson in popularity. Wanda's last movies were the 1927 productions Eyes of the Totem and Pirates of the Sky. Her career suddenly came to an end with the arrival of talkies.

THEY'RE STILL COOKIN' WITH GAS

March 22, 1998

It's not often that a Canadian company reaches the lofty age of 150, but that's exactly the plateau Toronto born Consumers' Gas will reach tomorrow. It was on that day, March 23, 1848, that the company's Act of Incorporation was passed by the legislative assembly of the Province of Canada, the latter being the name given to the union of Canada East and Canada West (now the provinces of Quebec and Ontario) that had taken place seven years earlier.

Gas manufacturing complex of Consumers' Gas at the Front and Parliament street intersection, c 1920. The building to the right of the view, at Front and Berkeley and opposite the Toronto *Sun*, is now the home of the Canadian Opera Company.

The company came about as a result of Torontonians' dissatisfaction with the way Mr. Albert Furniss was living up to his agreement. Furniss was a successful Montreal hardware merchant and the president of the Montreal Gaslight Company. In 1841 he had been awarded a contract to supply Toronto with its first gas streetlights. He erected a gas manufacturing plant on land leased from the city south of Front Street in a block on the bay bound by Berkeley on the east and Princes (now slightly misspelled as Princess) on the west.

In the plant quantities of coal delivered by schooners from across the lake were heated in iron retorts, and the gas that was driven off was directed to customers' houses through an underground piping system. With the opening of Furniss's new plant Toronto became the 11th city on the continent and 38th in the entire world to be able to boast it had its own gasworks. Not bad for a city that was just seven years old and had a population of less than 15 000.

Things got off to a great start when those first few lights began to glow on the night of December 28, 1841. One of the best-known admirers was novelist Charles Dickens who, while touring the Americas in 1842, stopped by our city. In his book *American Notes* he described Toronto as being "full of life and notion, bustle, business and improvement. The streets were well paved and lighted with gas."

As flattering as these comments may have been, it wasn't long before Furniss, who had decided to branch out into the water supply business as well, got himself into difficulties. With the limited resources available he couldn't do both properly and soon was receiving complaints from just about everyone. His gas customers were particularly upset, and it wasn't long before they took the extraordinary step of starting a rival company. As consumers of gas, the name of their new company was an easy choice. It would be called Consumers' Gas. The men chosen to nurture and guide the new enterprise represented an interesting cross-section of Toronto's fledgling business community. The postmaster was elected president, a wholesale druggist vice-president, and the publisher of the local newspaper, a couple of hardware and leather merchants, a tea importer, and a grocer served as directors. To round out the board, a hotel keeper and tavern owner (the latter a particularly important member of the community) were elected.

When the company received its official approval a century and a half ago tomorrow, one of the stated requirements in the incorporation document was that the company be up and running within five years. The board of directors, businessmen all, determined that the new company could do better than that, much better, in fact. Arrangements were made with a reticent but no doubt relieved Albert Furniss to purchase his original gas-manufacturing plant on the south side of Front Street. Within a few months of getting that official go-ahead, Consumers' Gas was in business. Now, 150 years later, the company is still going strong. Happy Birthday, Consumers' Gas.

Not long after this column appeared Consumers' Gas added the prefix Enbridge to its name. The company's original name had been selected in 1848 and had served well for a century and a half. However, with the company's recent diversification through the acquisition of various companies in the energy business, Consumers' Gas had evolved into a "bridge between energy companies." This energy bridge became Enbridge and today the company is known as Enbridge Consumers' Gas.

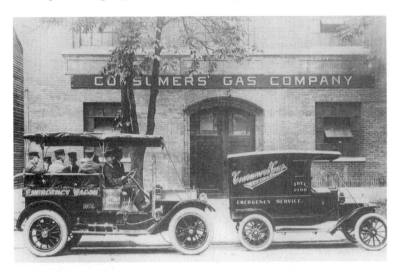

Consumers' Gas crew gets ready to roll in the company's Emergency Wagon #1, described as a 1914 Russell Depot Hack. It's parked behind one of the company's Model T Fords. Note the phone number, ADelaide 2180, reminiscent of a time when city phone numbers had prefixes instead of being all numbers. Remember yours?

BIG SHOTS BACK IN SHIPSHAPE

March 29, 1998

Just in case that much-talked-about tax revolt comes to pass, the government might want to look at adding the two old cannon resting outside the Queen's Park Crescent doors of the Whitney Block to its armoury. That way they'll have something to fend off the revolutionaries when they storm the bastion, just like the government forces had to when Mackenzie and the other rebels tried to take over our city back in 1837.

Le Prudent's cannons, before their restoration, take dead aim at the Parliament Buildings, 1998.

Now you're probably asking, What cannon is he talking about? Fair enough, for even though thousands of cars pass this pair of antique weapons each and every day as drivers make their way north on University Avenue, around the Parliament Buildings, and on up to Bloor Street, I don't imagine more than a few people are aware the guns are there. And thanks to some expert work by the people at the Canadian National Exhibition they'll be there for many more revolts to come.

But let's look at the history of the cannon. Research reveals that the pair had originally been part of the 74-gun complement on board the French warship *Le Prudent*. That vessel went to the bottom of Gabarus Bay after being sunk by British warships during the Siege of Louisburg in 1758. A century and a half passed before the pair were rescued from oblivion thanks to the efforts of the Canadian Club, who donated the guns to the government of the day.

John Rainford of the CNE's General Services Department examines *Le Prudent*'s recently refurbished cannons, both of which sit astride rebuilt carriages at their Queen's Park location.

However, another 20 years would pass before the then Minister of Highways, George S. Henry, a man who'd go on to serve as provincial Premier from 1930 to 1934, had the guns refurbished and given a place of prominence at Queen's Park. (Henry's remembered today in the name of a housing subdivision — Henry Farms — as well as a high school, both located in North York, his place of birth.)

As the years passed both cannon, as well as their wooden carriages, once again deteriorated, and it was obvious that once again something had to be done to preserve them. And here's where the CNE enters the picture. Several years ago, the two British cannon at the Fort Rouillé monument site in the Exhibition Grounds were refurbished by staff of the CNE's General Service's Department. Recognizing their expertise, government officials asked the CNE to quote on a similar project for them. Again the price was right, and work was soon underway to renew both carriages (using clear pine and the original hardware) and to refurbish the cannon barrels to ensure that rust and corrosion would not be a future concern. Earlier this week *Le Prudent*'s cannons were returned to Queen's Park.

The French warship *Le Prudent* burns off Louisburg during the siege of 1758. Two of her 74 cannons were recovered and now sit opposite the Parliament Buildings at Queen's Park (painting from the John Ross Robertson Collection at the Toronto Reference Library).

****

Sixty years ago yesterday, March 28, 1938, at the local Loblaw groceteria (and there's a word you don't hear any more), a pound of sirloin steak was selling for 27¢, ketchup, 12¢ a bottle, a dozen seedless oranges all the way from California for 19¢, exactly the same price as a large cauliflower. A six-quart basket of McIntosh apples (now we have Apple Macintoshes, as well) was selling for 39¢. And a pound of Pride of Arabia coffee was 27¢. A new Pontiac automobile was $895 and, while still on the subject of hard to believe, the Maple Leaf hockey team, under captain Syl Apps and with Turk Broda in goal, led Boston two games to none in the semi-finals. Looks like a Stanley Cup. Nope, not this year. Sure we beat the Bruins, but Chicago beat us three games to one in the finals. Ah, well, next year. It's always next year.

In the newspaper headlines that day 60 years ago, the Conservative Party leader R.B. Bennett, then in Opposition, declared that the country faced certain ruin unless harmony between the provinces was restored. He was speaking to the Ontario Secondary

Teachers Federation, and like a good politician tactfully added the motherhood-type statement, "No other people in the community have so large a responsibility and so great an obligation as teachers." In almost the same breath he managed to take a shot at the reigning Liberals and gave a pat on the head to a large group of voters. At the Casino theatre on the south side of Queen Street, just west of Bay, the stage show was something called *Spring Models of 1938*, and I don't think it featured cars. At the Imperial (later Imperial Six and now Pantages), Bette Davis starred in *Jezebel* while the Royal Alexandra featured the previous year's Pulitzer prize winning play *You Can't Take It With You*, but with the top ticket selling for two bucks, who cares.

Oh, there was something else that happened that March 28, 1938. The Canadian Cancer Society was established. Sixty years later its dedicated volunteers continue to raise funds and provide invaluable services to people living with cancer, their families and caregivers.

T.O. PAPER CARRIED TITANIC SCOOP

April 12, 1998

*T*itanic, one more time!

Next Wednesday marks the 86th anniversary of the sinking of mighty Royal Mail Steamer *Titanic*, and just when you think everything that can be said, written, or put into movie form about the ill-fated ship has been done, up pops another story. This time, though, it's a story that has a definite Toronto connection.

Several months ago I received a letter from Mildred Downey who enclosed an obituary notice that had run on January 18, 1960, in the *Daily Report*, an Ontario, California, newspaper. The subject of the obituary was Joseph A. Downey, Mildred's brother-in-law, a former reporter and an advertising man with that paper. Turns out as a young man Toronto born Downey worked in the newsroom of the old Toronto *World* newspaper at 40 Richmond Street West. The *World* was one of several morning papers and, as it would soon be proven, one of its most creative.

Early in the morning of Monday, April 15, 1912, as Downey and the boys were putting the finishing touches to that morning's copy of the *World*, a young reporter sat in a backroom idly monitoring the telegraph wire, much as the media monitor the police radio band today. Weather conditions were good and signals were flying. Suddenly, he was able to decipher amongst the various messages flashing through the ether frantic clicking that when translated turned out to be a personal message from a fortunate *Titanic* survivor informing someone, somewhere, of the disaster.

As the breathless reporter relayed the incredulous story to the *World*'s newsroom staff, the usually raucous room quickly fell silent. The story was unbelievable! Or was it just possible that the message untangled from that Morse code communiqué was really true? Could it be that the mighty RMS *Titanic*, the unsinkable *Titanic*, a towering example of man's ultimate conquest of nature and all the elements, assumed to be proudly ploughing her way across the Atlantic on her maiden voyage, was no more? The story was soon corroborated by a second intercepted wireless message, this one flashed to the offices of the Allan Line in Montreal by the captain of their passenger liner *Virginian*. He too reported that *Titanic* was in trouble and he was proceeding to her assistance.

Finally, someone recognized the immensity of the story that was breaking even as they collectively held their breath. But what should be done with it? That was the question. If the reports were false, some sort of ghoulish prank, say, and the paper was to report that the ship had gone down, the *World* would look foolish, painfully so with so many Canadians on board. But, if the story was true, the disaster would be, without question, the most important story any of them would ever work on.

These ads are taken from the Toronto *World* newspaper. The first appeared on Saturday, April 13, 1912, and shows scheduled trips for the mighty White Star sisters, *Olympic* and *Titanic*. As the ad shows, the ill-fated *Titanic* was due to depart New York City on April 20, 1912, for the return part of its maiden trip. That, of course, never happened. The same ad appeared in the *World* on Tuesday, April 16, with the reference to the younger sister deleted.

After much soul-searching, it was decided to go with the story as they had interpreted it. Soon everyone was assembling as much information on the White Star's new liner as possible. When the paper hit the streets shortly after 4:00 a.m. on the Monday morning (history would record that the *World* Extra appeared a mere two hours after the actual sinking), it was full of details about many of the famous passengers on board, salient facts about the new ship, and, most important, a bold statement that the ship was sinking and that women and children were being put off in the lifeboats.

The unfolding disaster still hadn't been confirmed, and virtually every other newspaper stated that although *Titanic* had indeed been involved in an accident there really was nothing to worry about. Some even reported that the mighty liner was safely under tow and headed for Halifax.

The Toronto *World* indeed had a scoop.

By the next day, Tuesday, April 16, 1912, what most people had at first believed impossible had finally been confirmed by White Star Line officials following receipt of a message from *Titanic*'s sister ship *Olympic*. With such confirmation all the world's newspapers were featuring the terrible story.

And while the *World*'s Tuesday morning edition featured a headline that screamed TITANIC SINKS; 1 800 PEOPLE DROWNED, the paper also managed to boast a little. On the front page, under a separate heading The *World* Never Sleeps, the paper explained how it alone had been the first to get the real story to its readers.

MICHIE'S TRADITION OF WEALTH AND PRESTIGE

April 19, 1998

George Forbes Michie, president of the company and grandnephew of the founder, George Michie.

There's nothing more satisfying than receiving a letter from one of my senior readers asking for a story on something they remember that was part of an older, less frantic Toronto. Often, their request is prompted by a newspaper or television story reporting on new developments planned for a site of which the reader has fond memories. Take Harold Wright's request, for instance. He saw the ad for a shiny new condominium tower planned for the former Nag's Head pub site at 5 King Street West. As bright and shiny as that new project, nicknamed by someone the Sliver Tower may turn out, for Harold Wright and many other Torontonians that King

Street address will always be remembered not as the home of the Nag's Head (that still exists in name in another Toronto location) but as the home of one of the city's best known businesses, Toronto's famous Michie and Company.

The Michie and Company store on King Street just west of Yonge can be seen in this turn-of-the-century photo. After Michie's closed, the building housed the Nag's Head Tavern for a time and is now the sales office of the new condominium planned for the site.

Michie's, a city institution that was to serve Torontonians for more than a century, first opened its doors in 1835 with George Michie waiting on his clients offering everything from stovepipes to pickles, from window glass to a dizzying array of wines and liquors. In fact, ancient company records reveal that the very first purchase, made shortly after Mr. Michie opened the shop door at what was then No. 7 King Street West was the sale of a hogshead (63 gallons) of gin for the sum of 12 pounds, 1 shilling and sixpence, the local currency still being based on that of mother England, to a Mr. William Gilmore.

Over the years, Michie and Company, Grocers and Wine Merchants, expanded its product line so that virtually anything the customer required was either in stock or could be ordered. This went for dry goods, building materials, food items (domestic or imported), wines, and liquors. The two latter items were deleted from the store's inventory following the passage of the Ontario Temperance Act in 1915. The sale of wines and liquors eventually became the responsibility of the province through its licensed stores, the first of which was located at the southeast corner of Church and Lombard streets.

The attention to store merchandise (an inventory that included such items as Valencia oranges, loaves of sugar, figs, rice, spices, ink, window glass, bitters, oatmeal, cognac and sherry, bread, and butter) as well as the company's insistence that service was as important as its huge inventory, quickly led to Michie's being the pre-eminent store of its type in all of Toronto. Michie's customers, whose names could be found in any book listing the country's Who's Who, made their way to the busy King and Yonge corner from all parts of the city and surrounding countryside. The transaction completed, servants would load the goods on wagons prior to the homeward trip to Rosedale, Parkdale, or Richmond Hill.

Soon after the death in 1947 of John Forbes Michie, the popular and respected owner of the business and grandnephew of the company founder George Michie, the business and good will of one the city's oldest companies was sold to the Robert Simpson Company.

Incidentally, something I learned while researching the history of Michie's was the derivation of the word *grocers*, as in the title Michie's, Grocers and Wine Merchants. In the company's early days a high-class grocer was often referred to as an "Italian warehouseman," someone who only handled rare spices and wines emanating from ports along the Mediterranean Sea. A grocer, on the other hand, was someone who was engrossed in a wide range of products. From the word *engrossed*, the word *grocer*.

TEMPORARY WAR TAX NOW ECONOMIC CORNERSTONE

April 26, 1998

Got your income tax done? You don't need me to tell you that the deadline for filing is midnight this coming Thursday. You know, I really think the government has taken this income tax idea too far. After all, when Sir Thomas White, the federal minister of finance in the Conservative government of Sir Robert Borden and the man who started the whole thing during the darkest days of the First World War, was asked how long the tax would be in force, he hinted that yes, it might be permanent. In his next sentence, however, he suggested that a "deliberate review" of the measure should be undertaken following the end of the war. I wonder if they ever did that?

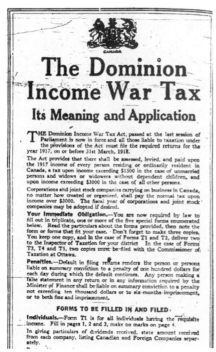

The government announced its new wartime income tax on March 9, 1918, using this newspaper notice.

In reality, the need to tax the general population became painfully clear when the amount of money being spent to finance a war that began in the summer of 1914 and was to be over by Christmas began escalating out of control. In fact, by the time the war had entered its third bloody year the federal government was faced with a mountain of bills directly attributable to the war effort that totalled more than $600 million. The government would have to get that money somewhere, and that somewhere was announced in late July, 1917, by Sir Thomas White, the minister of finance in Sir Robert Borden's Conservative government. The new Dominion Income Tax would require that unmarried men and widowers without children would pay a 4 percent tax on annual incomes exceeding $2 000 while all others would pay a similar percentage on incomes exceeding $3 000. Thus a bachelor earning $4 000 would pay $80 while a married man would hand over half that amount. There would also be a graduated super tax on incomes in excess of $6 000. This super tax would begin at 2 percent for incomes between $6 000 and $10 000, rising to 25 percent for incomes in excess of $100 000. It was estimated that in its first year, the new tax would raise somewhere between $15 and $20 million, all of which would go to write down the war debt. Filing of the necessary forms, a four-page T1 for individuals, T2s for corporations and joint stock companies, T3s for trustees, executors, administrators of estates, T4s by employers with the names of employees as well as amounts paid (from all sources) in excess of $1 000, and T5s by corporations with shareholders. The date for filing would be March 31, 1918. False statements could result in a fine not exceeding $10 000 or six months in jail. As history would prove, the annual rendezvous with the tax department had begun.

The *Evening Telegram* newspaper, never one to back away from a

Sir Thomas White, the father of federal income tax.

controversy, really got into the mood with a story that appeared on July 26, 1917. First the paper ensured everyone that women with incomes of their own would not escape under the new law. "There are more than a few in the city that have incomes exceeding the exempted

$2,000 and $3 000," the paper announced. The report went on to examine Sir William Mackenzie's financial status. As the owner of the city's privately run transportation system, Sir William was the target of many jabs. With the vast majority of streetcar riders failing to appreciate his street railway system, the article made great reading. In total, Mackenzie would pay municipal property tax on his residence, Benvenuto, on the Avenue Road hill, of $10 751 (the 1917 mill rate was 24), a municipal tax on income (don't tell today's politicians about this one) of $5 475, a provincial war tax of $623, plus the new Dominion Income Tax of $56 597. Mackenzie's total taxes — more than $70 000. The paper estimated there were at least 14 millionaires like Sir William in the city and with the multitude of loopholes available under the municipal income tax system, the new federal tax would mean they'd all pay their fair share, or so the newspaper surmised.

Next time we'll meet Sir Thomas White, the man who brought the country income tax.

MEET OUR FIRST TAXMAN

May 3, 1998

Now that your income tax is filed with the people up in Ottawa (it is, isn't it?) let's take a look at the man who started what's become an annual ritual, Sir Thomas White. As I pointed out in last week's column, the purpose of the new Dominion Income Tax was to help the federal government pay the enormous bills for wartime supplies that continued to spiral out of control as the Great War dragged on. Canadians began paying personal income tax on money earned in 1917 with that tax due by March 31, 1918. Hey, that was exactly 80 years ago. To celebrate the feds should have had a special anniversary discount. Nice idea, but...

39 Queen's Park Crescent East, the residence of Sir Thomas White, who introduced personal income tax in 1917.

The man Prime Minister Robert Borden tagged to bring in the new personal income tax was his minister of finance, Thomas White. White was born in Bronte, Ontario, in 1866 and educated in Oakville, Brampton, and here in Toronto, graduating from the U of T in 1895. He obtained a degree from Osgoode Hall, but never practiced, joining the newly established National Trust instead as its first general manager, rising over the next dozen years to become vice-president. Though a Liberal in political leanings, he differed with party leader Sir Wilfrid Laurier over the reciprocity issue and ran for the Progressive Conservatives in the 1911 federal election. He was successful, winning a seat in the House of Commons as representative for the County of Leeds. It was only natural that his work experience with National Trust would make him the ideal candidate as minister of finance, a position to which he was immediately appointed by Prime Minister Borden.

In 1917, Sir Thomas White (he had been knighted the previous year for his exemplary service as finance minister in the darkest days of the war) was re-elected. As the war entered its fourth year the monetary drain on the country had become more than anyone expected. Someone had to pay. That someone turned out to be the citizens, and on July 25, 1917, White introduced personal income tax across the land as a "temporary measure." In hindsight it seems old habits die hard.

While Borden was at the Paris peace conference White was acting prime minister, and while many believed he'd be the next party leader, White decided to retire from politics instead and joined the Bank of Commerce as vice-president. Soon after that he sold his house at 39 Queen's Park Crescent East, just north of St. Alban's (now Wellesley Street West), and moved to a beautiful new residence at 175 Teddington Park Avenue in north Toronto. White had built the house on the crescent opposite Queen's Park (the real park, not the legislative buildings everyone calls Queen's Park) shortly after the turn of the century, and though spending most of his time in Ottawa, this was his Toronto home when income tax was introduced.

Sir Thomas died February 11, 1955, and is buried in Mount Pleasant Cemetery.

**Some of the earliest settlers in this part of the world were members of the Ashbridge family, who arrived from Pennsylvania soon after Governor Simcoe visited the future site of Toronto in 1793. The Ashbridge clan included the mother, Sarah, two unmarried sons, one unmarried daughter, two of the married variety, plus their husbands and children. All in all quite a brood. This influx resulted in a sizeable increase in the area's population.

Today we know the Ashbridge name thanks to the continued existence of the Ashbridge house on Queen Street East, which has recently been turned over to the Ontario Heritage Foundation, as well as in the name of the body of water to the south of the old house. A new book, which documents the history of the area, has been published by the Toronto Ornithological Club. In it are stories and descriptions of the bay and environs prepared by such individuals from the past as Ely Playter, Lord Selkirk, Elizabeth Simcoe, and Ernest Thompson Seton, supplemented by stories prepared by a group of modern-day friends of the Bay. The book is titled, naturally enough, *Ashbridge's Bay.*

It may look like Tom Sawyer on the bank of the Mississippi River, but it's actually a couple of young Torontonians fishing in Ashbridge's Bay even as the Toronto Harbour Commission was redeveloping the area. That's one of the Commission's dredges in the background.

THEY'RE TORONTO'S OWN GUIDING LIGHTS

May 10, 1998

The Queen's Wharf lighthouse was moved to its present location on Lake Shore Blvd. W. in late 1929.

I belong to a number of special interest organizations that have some aspect of Canadian history as a common denominator. Each of them publishes a newsletter, one of the most interesting being that of the Canadian Aviation Historical Society. Here's an excerpt from the most recent edition documenting a radio conversation between a U.S. Navy warship off the coast of Newfoundland and Canadian authorities. It's been confirmed that this dialogue really took place.

Americans: Please divert your course 15 degrees to the north to avoid collision.

Canadians: Recommend you divert *your* course 15 degrees to the south to avoid a collision.

Americans: This is the captain of a U.S. navy ship. I say again, divert *your* course!

Canadians: No, I say again, you divert *your* course.

Americans: This is the aircraft carrier USS *Abraham Lincoln*, the second largest ship in the United States' Atlantic fleet. We are accompanied by 3 destroyers, 3 cruisers and numerous support vessels. I demand that you change your course 15 degrees north, that's one five degrees north or countermeasures will be taken to ensure the safety of this ship!

Canadians: This is a lighthouse...your call!

And speaking of lighthouses — nice segue, eh? — we have a couple of them right here in Toronto: the Gibraltar Point lighthouse on Toronto Island plus the Queen's Wharf lighthouse on Lake Shore Boulevard West, right in front of the former Molson Brewery building.

While the former is still in its original location, the latter isn't. The Queen's Wharf lighthouse was moved from the northeast corner of the busy Bathurst Street, Fleet Street, and Lake Shore Boulevard

The lighthouse in its original location close to the old Western Gap.

The old lighthouse gets higher and drier as crews fill in the old Western Gap.

intersection in 1929, where it sat high and dry for many years. The original purpose of this lighthouse, and the reason it had been erected in 1861 at the end of the old Queen's Wharf, was to guide shipping into the safety of Toronto Harbour. When a new, safer Western Gap was excavated several hundred yards to the south of the old gap in 1911, the battered lighthouse was without a job. Somehow, somebody thought to keep the relic, and it was dragged by a team of horses over a series of wooden rollers to its present location. Its preservation is now the responsibility of Heritage Toronto.

WHAT'S IN A NAME? PLENTY

May 17, 1997

A July, 1923, view of the corner of Third Avenue and Broadway. Where? Nope, not in Toronto, but in Yorkton, Saskatchewan.

I recently received a request from the city of Yorkton, Saskatchewan, for help in locating some early history of their community. Actually, the idea of asking us for information about the early days of their city isn't as far-fetched as one would at first think. Especially when you realize that the name Yorkton starts with the same word, York, that Lieutenant Governor John Simcoe gave to our community in 1793. (The original name *Toronto* was reapplied when we became a city in 1834.) York was also the name of the surrounding county that had been created by Simcoe one full year earlier.

The County of York was one of 19 established throughout the new Province of Upper Canada (Ontario after 1867) and came into being for a couple of reasons. The first allowed for the creation of a specific electoral division for governmental and administrative purposes, while the second permitted the formation of a militia force for the protection of the governor's new province.

Now, you may ask, what has all this to do with the naming of a community out in western Canada? When British Columbia entered

Confederation in 1871, it was promised a rail connection with the rest of the country. To fulfil this promise the government agreed to finance the construction of the new line, which was to be built by the recently established CPR. As the rails made their way westward, mass migration followed, and here's where the Yorkton story begins. The job of surveying the Assiniboia area, a huge tract of land that included a large part the modern province of Saskatchewan, began in 1882, just one year after the CPR was incorporated. Even as the survey parties were arriving to divide up the land, numerous land colonization companies were being formed back east. These companies would bid for various parcels of land, subdivide the purchase further, then sell those lots to eager settlers.

One such enterprise was established in Toronto in 1882 after its three founding members, James Armstrong, J.J. Cooke, and R.N. Taylor, had travelled west, first by steam train as far as Winnipeg, then by oxcart to a farming district not far from the site of the present City

Born in York County, Ontario, James Armstrong was the father of Yorkton, Saskatchewan.

of Yorkton. When they got there, they liked what they saw. On their return to Toronto the trio opened an office at 1 Victoria Street where stock in the new company as well as parcels of land were offered for sale. As the three principals were all residents of communities scattered throughout the still rural County of York (as were most of the company's first customers), the venture was naturally enough given the name York Farmers' Colonization Company.

Sales were brisk, and people quickly relocated to the new western settlement. As it grew in size and population, the community underwent several name changes. At first it was simply the York Colony, an obvious reference to the county from which most of the setters had emigrated. Next came the rather grandiose title York City, and when that didn't stick, the name Yorkton was adopted. In all cases the York County connection was maintained.

But, while the name Yorkton stuck, the original townsite didn't. So influential and important was the railway, the town fathers decided to relocate the pioneer community two miles to the south where it would be adjacent to an all-important rail line that connected the thriving communities of Portage La Prairie, Manitoba, and Saskatoon. This new location became the site of the modern Yorkton, a city that today has a population in excess of 15 000, covers 5 700 acres, has 23 churches, 5 public and 3 separate elementary schools, 1 public and 1 separate high school, and a regional college.

THE SINKING OF A CANADIAN DREAM

May 24, 1998

Artist William Wheeler's dramatic painting depicts the *Empress* seconds before she slipped beneath the cold waters of the St. Lawrence River. Courtesy Salvation Army Heritage Centre.

There's probably not a person in the entire civilized world that hasn't heard about the ill-fated RMS *Titanic*. Countless books and newspaper and magazine articles have been written about the ship's tragically short existence, which ended on the morning of April 16, 1912. And, as I understand it, a movie was released recently that also deals with the *Titanic* story.

And while millions around the world know all about *Titanic*, I'll bet only an infinitesimally small percentage of them have ever heard about a similarly appalling disaster that befell a great Canadian ship, the CPR liner *Empress of Ireland*. Perhaps that's because our disaster didn't occur during the vessel's maiden voyage. And while the *Empress* had a few millionaires and well-known people listed on her passenger manifest, those numbers came nowhere near the Who's Who on board *Titanic*.

Titanic's collision with the iceberg was well out to sea, at a location remote from any potential rescue ships. On the other hand, the *Empress* tragedy, also the result of a collision, took place not in the wide expanse of some ocean, but right in our own St. Lawrence River a mere 200 or so miles downstream from its point of departure, Quebec City, and just a couple of miles from the pretty community of Rimouski.

Without question, the death toll associated with *Titanic*'s sinking was appalling, but when one compares the number of passengers lost on each of the vessels, the true magnitude of the *Empress of Ireland* tragedy becomes more apparent. *Titanic* was a much larger ship with a far greater number of passengers and crew on board. While *Titanic* lost 807 of her passengers, in cold hard facts 61 percent, the *Empress* lost 840 passengers, or a horrific 80 percent. From this it can be seen that more passengers died in the Canadian disaster than in the sinking of *Titanic*, or of the next-best-known marine disaster, the sinking of the Cunard liner *Lusitania*, torpedoed off the south coast of Ireland on May 7, 1915, with the loss of 791 passengers. This dubious distinction remains little known and is an incredibly sad fact.

But now, thanks to David Zeni, retired U.S. Navy officer turned author, that should change. His magnificently written and illustrated *Forgotten Empress* finally pays tribute to Canada's worst marine disaster.

In his book Zeni relates the story in great detail, commencing with the creation of the Canadian Pacific Railway in the 1880s and the company's decision to make the enterprise an intermodal transportation system consisting of steamships and rolling stock that would stretch from the great cities of Europe across Canada and all the way to Japan.

After a moving ceremony at Mutual Arena in downtown Toronto some of the members of the Salvation Army who perished in the disaster are laid to rest in Mount Pleasant Cemetery. The impressive *Empress of Ireland* memorial was dedicated in 1916.

The railway was completed in late 1885 with transcontinental passenger service inaugurated in June of the following year. Before long the CPR was busily engaged in the second half of the dream, steamship service across the Atlantic and Pacific oceans. The company began its shipping service close to home on the Great Lakes with the *Alberta, Athabasca,* and *Algoma,* the first members of what would become an immense fleet of passenger ships. Soon more craft were added, with several of the most beautiful, *Empress of India, Empress of China,* and *Empress of Japan,* all bearing the prefix that was to identify vessels of the great white fleet. And on June 29, 1906, the proud Canadian pacific fleet grew once more with the arrival of *Empress of Ireland* fresh from the Fairfield Shipbuilding Works in Glasgow, Scotland.

As the years passed the *Empress of Ireland* gained a strong reputation for being a safe ship, something more than a few people had in mind when they selected her for their May 28, 1914, passage to England. On board for that particular trip were 171 Salvation Army members, many from Toronto, bound for the Army's third international conference in London, England.

Toronto Sketches 6

The ship got underway at 4:27 that afternoon, and soon the sleek vessel was gliding downstream, next stop Liverpool. Shortly before 2:00 the following morning, crew of the *Empress* saw the navigation lights of an inbound ship off to the starboard (right). The ship was still almost two miles away. Remaining on their present course the two would pass starboard to starboard. Suddenly, the *Empress* was enveloped in thick fog, and the other ship vanished. Audible signals between the two craft continued, but something wasn't right. The sound of other vessel's horn became louder. Where was she? Suddenly the fog cleared just in time for Captain Kendal to watch in horror as the bow of the heavily laden coal carrier *Storstad* sliced into his ship. In less than 15 minutes the *Empress of Ireland* was no more. Gone were 1 014 of her 1 492 passengers and crew.

Each year on the Sunday closest to May 29, the day the *Empress* sank, the Salvation Army holds a public service of remembrance at the *Empress of Ireland* memorial just inside Mount Pleasant Cemetery's Yonge Street gate. There's also a display of *Empress of Ireland* artifacts on view at the Salvation Army Heritage Centre, 2130 Bayview Avenue, North York.

TORONTO'S STORMY PAST

May 31, 1998

Looking for a reason to party this afternoon? Why not throw an impromptu bash, not for someone you know, but for a place I'm sure you've all visited, Toronto Island. Incidentally, since it consists of more than 20 islands, large and small, it should really be Toronto Islands, but I won't buck tradition — Toronto Island it is.

The reason for the party? It was on this very day, May 31, 1858, precisely 140 years ago, that two ships, *Eliza* and *Highland Chief,* sailed through the recently created Eastern Gap, whose formation a few weeks earlier had resulted in the creation of Toronto Island. (Actually, the birth of the Island took place the previous April 13, so that date would have been more appropriate for a 140th anniversary party, but it was still too cool.)

In our city's early days, Toronto Harbour was enclosed by a peninsula, closed in except for a narrow opening at its western end. In the 1850s that all changed when savage storms intermittently breached the narrow isthmus at the east end where the peninsula was connected to the mainland. Then on April 13, 1858, a particularly nasty storm hit the young city, resulting in torrential outflows from the area rivers. Water from the Don River permanently breached the narrow isthmus at the east end of the peninsula, leaving a gaping 500-foot channel.

With the creation of this Eastern Gap, the peninsula was suddenly and permanently transformed into Toronto Island. And while the gap would try to heal itself by frequently silting up, a concerted effort was made to keep it open. However, a permanent navigable passageway, complete with protective side walls, didn't come into existence until the federal and municipal governments finally came to terms nearly four decades later.

Upgrading of that turn-of-the-century construction project is obvious in the look of today's Eastern Gap.

Let's go back to that ancient peninsula for a moment. As old as it was when the isthmus was breached on this day 140 years ago, it wasn't always a part of our geography. In fact, its presence is due to the Scarborough Bluffs several miles to the east.

It was a combination of the continual erosion of the Bluffs and the westerly flow of water on the north side of Lake Ontario that resulted in the eroded material being carried towards the future site of Toronto Island. Opposite this site, the outflow from the Don and Humber rivers caused the currents to slow allowing the suspended material to settle forming what at first were described as "feathery whisps of land." Over time this formation grew into substantial sandbars.

Postcard views of Toronto Island were popular souvenirs at the turn of the century.

With the addition of material dredged from the harbour bottom and the nearby river mouths, plus street sweepings and construction riprap from the city, the Island grew from 360 acres in 1879, to 563 in 1912, and eventually to its present 820 acres.

AN IMPORTANT CORNER IN TORONTO'S HISTORY

June 7, 1998

Yonge Street looking north to the Carlton Street corner (right) and, farther north and on the left, the College Street corner, 1915. Note the IOOF Hall in the distance, and farther up Yonge Street the tower of old No. 3 firehall. Though the firehall has moved around the corner, the old tower is still there.

Ever wondered why one of the city's major crosstown streets has two completely different names, College to the west of Yonge and Carlton to the east? In an attempt to end this confusion, over the years there have been several attempts to choose one or other of the names for the entire thoroughfare. Needless to say, those attempts failed, and a good thing, too, since both names have special connections with our community's history.

Prior to the early 1930s, College Street, which recognizes old King's College the 1843 forerunner of the modern University of Toronto, which occupied a building that stood where the Parliament Buildings are today, actually formed a T intersection where the thoroughfare met Yonge Street. In its earliest days, this dirt pathway was first known by the rather grandiose title of The College Avenue, leading as it did to and from King's College. It was considered a private road with access controlled by a gatehouse at Yonge Street. (A second College Avenue, connecting the college with Queen Street to the south, was also private, with a portion going into the alignment of today's University Avenue.)

For years after the creation of the new (and present) University of Toronto in 1850, College Avenue (eventually renamed College Street) remained under the control of the U of T, as did a portion of University Avenue, until both were deeded to the city for certain considerations.

Several storefronts south of the intersection, and on the opposite side of the street, was the start of Carlton Street, which ran east to Parliament Street. The name Carlton recognizes Guy Carleton Wood, the brother of Ann McGill (McGill Street), who was the wife of Rev. John Strachan (Strachan Avenue), the Anglican bishop of Toronto from 1839 to 1867 and owner of property in the area. Note that we continue to misspell Carlton.

The 1892 Independent Order of Oddfellows Hall still stands at the northwest of College and Yonge streets. Starbucks now takes the place the CIBC's bucks.

Originally, streetcars on the Carlton route had to navigate the awkward and dangerous jog at Yonge Street in a manner shown in a 1915 photo.

As the Great Depression of the late 1920s and early 1930s deepened, it was decided to eliminate the jog as part of a citywide works program. On June 4, 1931, following the demolition of several buildings and the laying of new sidewalks, roadbeds, tracks, and curves, streetcar and vehicular traffic began using the present College and Carlton alignment.

Visible in the old photo at the northwest corner of College and Yonge streets is a building that has watched over the corner for more than a century. Information obtained from Heritage Toronto reveals that this mini medieval castle was built for the Independent Order of Oddfellows' Hall in 1891 to a design prepared by prominent Toronto architects Norman Dick and Frank Wickson. It was here, in special rooms and meeting halls on the upper floors, that the IOOF's Canada Lodge No. 49 held its secret, and often mystical, meetings for many years. Another tenant from the day the building opened in 1892 was the Bank of Commerce, which closed, as a branch of the CIBC, only recently. The location is now occupied by a Starbucks coffee shop.

A STREETCAR NAMED PETER WITT

July 5, 1998

Recently, in a letter to the editor in one of our city newspapers, a reader suggested that Toronto replace its streetcars on the busy Queen Street route with natural gas buses. While the logistics of accommodating the immense number of passengers who ride the high-capacity Articulated Light Rail Vehicles in service on the city's busiest surface line on a fleet of low-capacity, difficult-to-procure buses is staggering, many of the follow-up letters to the editor comment on the place the streetcar has in the look of our city. In fact, some suggested that streetcars, like police officers on horses and the Toronto Island ferryboats, were some of the things that made our city the special place it is.

Historically, streetcars in a variety of forms have been part of the cityscape since the first horse-drawn vehicles were introduced in 1861. The entire system was converted using the wonder of the age,

Cleveland Transit commissioner and streetcar designer Peter Witt (1869–1948).

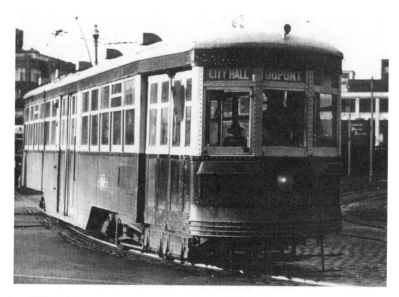

Small Witt # 2766 exits the loop at Christie and Dupont streets on its way downtown on the Bay route (photo courtesy Ted Wickson).

electricity, during the period 1892 to 1894. With the creation of the TTC in 1921, the most modern variety of streetcar then available quickly supplanted the older wooden cars. They were identified as Peter Witts, after the Cleveland, Ohio, transit official who designed the car. Toronto's streetcar fleet consisted of two versions of Witt's design, the large Witt, which was nearly 52 feet in length, and the small Witt, slightly shorter at 47 feet.

Over the years the TTC operated 250 of the former, 100 of the latter, plus 225 of the unpowered Witt trailer, which tagged along behind the large Witt cars on the busiest streetcar routes. Of this number only one small Witt remains on the TTC's streetcar roster.

Witt #2766 was built in late 1922 and went into service exactly 75 years ago. As newer equipment was acquired, the Witt equipment was retired, with the last large Witt exiting in 1961 and the last small Witt two years later. All but a few were scrapped, with several donated to transit museums such the Halton County Radial Railway museum west of Toronto.

Somehow old #2766 survived the purge. Discussions are underway to have the car operate as a part of a sightseeing service along with a pair of 1950-vintage PCC Streamliners still owned by the Commission.

In the spring of 2000, the PCCs returned to charter service. The Peter Witt will have to wait its turn.

Peter Witt 2610 reaches the end of the line, c. 1954.

BRIDGING THE GAP TO THE DANFORTH

July 12, 1998

Several weeks ago I wrote about the reason one of the city's major east-west thoroughfares has two names, Carlton east of Yonge and College to the west. On the subject of confusing street names, there's another crosstown thoroughfare that is also identified by two different names, Bloor Street and Danforth Avenue, or as the latter is more often called, the Danforth. (Why? I have no idea.)

Passengers board the elevated at Bloor and Bay. Actually, a picture of a German elevated train was trimmed and pasted (literally — there weren't any computers to do that work back then) onto a photo of the busy Toronto corner. The people waiting to board are Germans, those on the street Torontonians.

This time the reason for the street's two titles is easier to understand. Until the connecting link, consisting of a long earthen embankment and two concrete and steel bridges, was completed in 1918, these streets were separated by a couple of major geographical impediments, the deep ravine east of Sherbourne Street and the vast valley of the Don River. The gap approached nearly a mile and a half in length.

Work is well underway on the eastern section of the new viaduct that would span the valley of the Don River, 1916.

This view of the Prince Edward Viaduct is well known to drivers on the Don Valley Parkway and Bayview Extension, 1998.

Historically, the idea of connecting the city with the remote Danforth area had been put forward on several occasions in the late 1800s, but it was all talk. Years went by before anything concrete (and steel) was done, and while the structures were originally referred to, collectively, as simply the Bloor-Danforth viaduct, an automobile trip over the bridge by the Prince of Wales during his visit to the city in August, 1919, changed that. The royal trip quickly prompted city council to rename the $2 480 349 project (it came in $19 650.95 under budget) the Prince Edward Viaduct, a name that remains as its official title.

Following the suggestion of a Chicago based consulting firm, designers incorporated into the Don Valley section of the viaduct provision for a future tube (subway) line. It's a well-known piece of Toronto history trivia that the foresightedness shown those many years ago resulted in a huge savings when it came time to cross the valley with the Bloor-Danforth subway line in 1966.

Bloor Street was also the location for another proposal to improve public transit. This time it was to be an elevated rapid transit line soaring over the north side of Bloor. This 1958 scheme was quickly derailed, but not before a hastily prepared mock-up photo was made and run in the evening papers.

ROY ROGERS' HAPPY TRAILS LED TO TORONTO

July 19, 1998

When I was a kid growing up in a much less sophisticated Toronto, it wouldn't have been a typical Saturday afternoon without that expedition to the local movie house to take in rip-roarin', knock-em-down, ridin' and ropin' cowboy movies. At first, living near Bathurst and Bloor, I had a choice of the nearby Alhambra, Midtown, Bloor, or Metro theatres, and when the family moved to North Toronto, that quartet was replaced by the Circle and Capitol (both on Yonge Street), the little Mt. Pleasant, and the Belsize. And once I was in my teens, I'd often travel a little further afield to see something special playing at the Park, Fairlawn, Avenue, or Eglinton. Often that something special was a Roy Rogers flick. Sure, Gene Autry, Whip Wilson, Red Rider, and the Durango Kid were OK, but there was only one Roy Rogers. And like that less sophisticated Toronto of years gone by, Roy too is now part of history.

Some horseplay during Roy and Trigger's visit to Maple Leaf Gardens on May 2, 1944. Note the fellows and gals in uniform. The war still had more than a year to go.

Actually, Roy played an interesting part in one of the most memorable incidents in Toronto's history, for it was Roy Rogers who introduced tiny Marilyn Bell to the thousands who attended the CNE Grandstand show the evening after the 16-year-old Toronto schoolgirl completed her 21-hour crossing of Lake Ontario. Roy was the headliner at the 1954 Ex and was accompanied by wife Dale Evans, the Sons of the Pioneers, Trigger, Trigger Jr., plus eight performing Liberty palomino horses.

This wasn't Roy's first public appearance in our city. In a newspaper story that appeared during his 1944 visit as the headliner of the five-day Texas Rodeo Show at Maple Leaf Gardens, he confirmed that this was his fifth trip to our city. Not bad when you realize that Roy didn't really become a star until the late 1930s.

The King of the Cowboys returned to star at the 1954 CNE Grandstand Show and again in 1959 to make a special guest appearance at the Royal Agricultural Winter Fair. Roy Rogers died July 6, 1998.

Ten years later Roy and Dale played the CNE Grandstand. On August 26, 1954, they arrived at Toronto's Malton Airport (now Pearson International), where they accepted the keys to the car they'd use during their stay.

** A couple of compact discs have recently been released, and both have interesting connections with our city. The first is titled *More Lost Recordings* and contains 14 songs performed by the

Canadian Band of the Allied Expeditionary Force (AEF) led by Toronto born Robert Farnon. This band, which was organized by Farnon here in Toronto in the spring of 1944, was the Canadian counterpart of the America Band of the AEF led by the legendary Glenn Miller. In fact, when Miller failed to show up to lead his band as part of a London–Paris radio hook-up, it was Farnon's band that stepped in to keep the show going. Miller was never seen again. Farnon, who was recently awarded the Order of Canada, was born on July 24, 1917, in a house that still stands at 96 Woodside Avenue in west Toronto.

The second CD is a pair of discs released in this, the centennial year of the birth of the immortal George Gershwin. Titled, appropriately enough, *George Gershwin Memorial Concert*, the set features selections from the special concert performed at the Hollywood Bowl not long after Gershwin's death on July 11, 1937. Performing Gershwin classics are Al Jolson, Fred Astaire, Oscar Levant, and Lily Pons. The producers of this important addition to the Gershwin library are Torontonians David Lennick and Greg Gormick. Interestingly, Gershwin appeared at Toronto's Massey Hall on January 19, 1934, as part of a tour that was advertised as being "restricted to America's 30 leading music centres." Seems even back then Toronto was a recognized music hotbed. In the newspaper ads for that concert Gershwin was described as a "famed modern composer-pianist" with tickets priced from $1.00 to $2.50. Apparently, the money he earned from these concerts allowed him to go into semi-retirement while he composed the music for *Porgy and Bess*. I highly recommend both these recordings.

BRIDGE TO CANADA'S SUPERHIGHWAYS

July 26, 1998

When George S. Henry, Ontario's Minister of Highways, cut the ribbon to officially open the new bridge that soared over the valley of the Don River a little to the northwest of the small community of Hogg's Hollow, little did he know that this 1920s engineering triumph would someday become an integral part of one of Canada's future superhighways.

As soon as Ontario's pioneer settlers began using Yonge Street, a thoroughfare that had been slashed through the forests by Governor Simcoe's Rangers, they faced problems negotiating the hill into and out of the ravine cut through the landscape by the west branch of the Don River. We now call this ravine Hogg's Hollow.

It was on this fork of the Don that some of the area's earliest mills were erected, and it was because of these mills, located several miles north of the Town of York (Toronto's name from 1793 until 1834) in York township, that the nearby community was first named York Mills.

A prominent member of this ancient Toronto suburb was Scottish born James Hogg, who became one of the community's first millers. When James died in 1839, his sons John and William carried on the milling operations started by their father and soon began investing their hard earned money in land acquisition throughout the valley. As described in her fine book *Pioneering in North York*, Patricia Hart relates that sometime in the mid-1850s the boys hired a Toronto firm of surveyors and requested the company to draw up a plan of building lots in what the brothers described as "the Village of York Mills otherwise known as Hogg's Hollow." In the first advertisement for a development scheme in suburban Toronto, the Hoggs described the venture in these words:

The village possesses many privileges and advantages to induce families to purchase and settle, viz: - Three resident clergymen, an experienced physician, several churches in the village and neighbourhood, a good brick schoolhouse, stores, post office, two extensive flour mills in operation, in the hands of Capitalists, and in course of erection by the Proprietors, who have a steam saw mill and brick yard in full operation affording every facility to purchasers for building. Three omnibuses run through the village daily to and from the city, one carrying the daily mail.

The steep hill into Hogg's Hollow is obvious in this photo looking south towards the city from in front of the ancient Jolly Miller tavern. The radial streetcar tracks can be seen in the dust to the right of this c 1915 photo.

It would appear that Hugh Heron has nothing on the Hogg boys.

While the Hogg boys praised their development in glowing terms, there was a major drawback: the steep hills into and out of the hollow that became impassable at certain times of the year. In winter snow made the hills slippery slopes. Spring rains did the same thing. Heavy loads usually required additional teams of horses.

One way around the problem was to skirt the ravine. Traffic would use the streets we today identify as Donwoods Drive, Ivor Crescent, and Old Yonge Street. Obviously as this traffic increased in numbers and size of vehicles, this particular detour became less than satisfactory.

The real answer was the construction of a new road and a bridge across the valley. First came the new thoroughfare. It angled off Yonge Street at the city limits in a northwesterly direction, then curved northeasterly, where it connected with a mammoth new bridge, initially called the Yonge Boulevard Viaduct, which soared over the valley of the Don. A short extension at the north end of the bridge connected the boulevard with Yonge Street well north of the problem ravine. The problem was solved.

Work on the viaduct began in early 1928, and on January 5, 1929, the 1 225-foot-long structure was officially opened by Highways Minister George Henry. The roadway was 54 feet wide with 7-foot-wide sidewalks on either side. It was anticipated that someday streetcar tracks would be laid down the middle of the viaduct's roadbed. The total expenditure for the concrete and steel bridge and connecting roadways approached $1 million.

The 1929 Yonge Boulevard Viaduct over the west branch of the Don River is visible in the background as this North Yonge Railways radial car heads south into Hogg's Hollow from its northern terminus in Richmond Hill c 1934.

In December 1952, when the 1.8-mile stretch of the new Toronto By-pass Highway finally opened to traffic, it incorporated the old Yonge Boulevard viaduct. Exactly 13 years later the section from Yonge Street to Highway 400 became 12 lanes wide, still incorporating the original Yonge Boulevard viaduct where it crosses the Don Valley.

Today, what was the Toronto By-pass Highway is Highway 401, the Macdonald-Cartier Freeway. And while *freeway* is part of the modern name, if a recommendation made back in 1956 had been approved, Highway 401 would be a toll road.

ON THE RIGHT TRACK

August 2, 1998

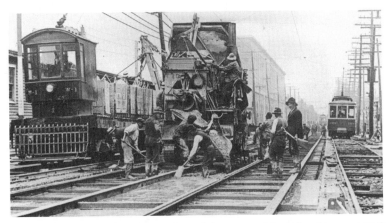

Track work on Queen Street East in front of the now vanished Woodbine race track (the grandstand in the background was recently demolished). This 1921 project resulted in a temporary track being laid in the curb lane on the north side of the street on which a service car can be seen headed downtown.

I'm always intrigued when ideas from the dim, dark past are revived for use in today's modern world. Take, for instance, something the TTC has recently acquired. It's called a temporary turnout and is used to permit streetcars to pass trackwork repairs that would normally interrupt the flow of traffic on the line. In many cases, such repair work necessitates the diversion of streetcars around the scene, with a resulting serious disruption in service. And depending on the location of the repair work and the unavailability of nearby streets with tracks onto which the streetcars can be diverted, buses may have to be substituted. If it's a busy route, the inability of buses to cope with large crowds can result in major deterioration of service.

The Commission's newly acquired temporary turnout, which will be used for the first time next month as part of repair work on Gerrard Street, is a simple but ancient idea. Some cities began using the concept decades ago. Here's how the turnouts — since they are used in pairs — work. They look like portable track switches, like those found at street intersections. One turnout is placed in front of the piece of track under repair; the other is placed at the end of the repair. With the turnouts in place a streetcar is able to slowly switch onto the adjacent track, operate over it in the wrong direction, and then divert back to the proper track once the repair area has been passed.

When the centre-of-the-road streetcar right-of-way on St. Clair Avenue West between Bathurst and Dufferin was replaced in 1928, streetcars were forced to use diversion tracks laid along the south side of the street. This photo was taken near Christie Street.

Of course all this is done with proper regard for streetcars operating in the opposite direction and with the assistance of traffic safety personnel. Oh, and someone has to switch the trolley pole. Recent experiments on Wychwood Avenue have proved the viability of these turnouts. Mark another victory for old technology.

While I've been unable to find instances of temporary turnouts here in Toronto, there are lots of references to similar pieces of equipment used in American cities years ago. Perhaps we're just catching up. And while we didn't use this particular piece of equipment (at least I haven't found anything yet), Toronto did have something similar that was used when a fire necessitated the laying of hose across the tracks.

It was called a hose jumper and consisted of two lengths of track bent up and over a small tube-like opening. The jumper was clamped to the track, fire hoses were slipped through the tube opening, and firemen went about fighting the fire. Meanwhile, the streetcars rode up and over the hoses, and service was maintained.

Photos of hose jumpers in use are impossible to find, but I did come across a couple of views of major track rebuilding projects of the past and resulting streetcar diversions. The Queen Street work was one of the first projects undertaken by the newly established TTC.

A modern TTC streetcar negotiates a temporary turnout during a test on Wychwood Avenue in May 1998.

TRAFFIC STOPPERS

August 9, 1998

The now familiar electric traffic signal, with its trio of red, amber, and green lights arranged vertically, was introduced in 1926. Toronto's very first electric signal had been installed at Yonge and Bloor the previous year. However, unlike the signal in this photo, it had its lights arranged horizontally.

Boy, these red light runners are certainly a pain in the gas, and am I wrong or are their numbers increasing? You know, there was a time when we didn't have to worry about this type of inconsiderate and often dangerous driver, a time when there weren't any red light runners at all. In fact, I can confirm that prior to August 8, 1925, exactly 73 years ago yesterday, there wasn't a red light runner to be found around town. Why? Because up until that day there wasn't a red traffic light anywhere in all of Toronto. To be sure, there wasn't a traffic light of any kind anywhere in the entire city. It wasn't until August 8, 1925, that the very first traffic signal flashed on at the corner of Yonge and Bloor streets.

A Toronto policeman using a semaphore, the latest in traffic regulating equipment, is seen on duty at the busy Yonge and Queen intersection in the early 1920s.

Unlike the modern-day traffic signals (of which there are nearly 1 800) the red, yellow (now orange), and green lights were placed horizontally with just one set facing approaching traffic. For the first few days, constables were stationed at the intersection to operate the signal as well as to explain what each coloured signal meant to those who couldn't understand the new strategy introduced to try to keep cars from slamming into each other or into jittery pedestrians. After this trial period, drivers were supposed to stop when the signal turned red. And, as I understand it, they're still supposed to.

That pioneer automatic traffic signal at Yonge and Bloor wasn't the first time police tried to regulate traffic. As early as 1913 an attempt to warn drivers that they were approaching an intersection, and the possibility of vehicular cross-traffic, was instituted on College Street between Yonge and Spadina. Blue lights were installed on the corner hydro poles, but the experiment was less than successful. Cars still ran into other cars.

On June 1, 1920, Toronto Police Chief Dickson instituted what had become a highly successful traffic regulator in the States, the semaphore. This piece of equipment, consisting of *stop* and *go* signs atop a metal pole, the positioning of which could be controlled by the officer, was placed in the centre of an intersection as the volume of traffic required. Using the semaphore and hand signals, the helmeted officer attempted to take charge of the traffic. His job was made somewhat easier when a hand-pump-activated whistle and kerosene lamp illuminating red and green coloured glass bull's-eyes on top of the signal were added some time later.

The semaphore was a frequent sight at busy corners for the next half decade or so until the first traffic light appeared at Yonge and Bloor. In November, 1926, automatic signals of the vertical style were installed to control major intersections in the King, Victoria, Dundas, Bay part of downtown.

Attempts to better control vehicle traffic continued over the years and in the summer of 1930 one of the most unusual was the installation of car-horn-activated signals at the corner of busy Yonge Street and the little used Chatsworth Drive in north Toronto. Approaching Yonge Street, a car on Chatsworth would toot its horn, and eventually the light opposite would change, permitting the driver to cross. The signal had been in operation only a short time when it was noticed that traffic on Yonge would often be congested in the vicinity of Chatsworth while there was no cross traffic in sight. Staking out the corner, police soon discovered a playful pedestrian with little else to do, shouting "Hello! Hello!" at the light. Somehow his voice mimicked a car horn, and the light changed. Police suggested he find some other way to entertain himself.

ALL ABOARD FOR A TRIP INTO THE PAST

August 16, 1998

Recently, there have been reports in the media concerning the proposed addition of sound barriers adjacent to the Canadian Pacific Railway's rail line that passes through the north end of Rosedale, and the potential negative impact that installation will have on houses along Summerhill Avenue. The controversy isn't new, for over the years the presence of this busy railway right-of-way in a populated area has been the subject of various and sundry complaints from nearby residents. Of course, such concerns were non-existent when the line was cut through virtual wilderness back in the mid-1880s. Its location, well north of the city limits of the day, was between the Town of Yorkville (which would become part of the city about the same time the right-of-way was being cleared) and the remote suburban community of Deer Park farther north, which spread out around the dusty intersection of Yonge Street and St. Clair Avenue.

Looking south on Yonge Street to the CPR underpass at Birch Avenue in 1946. Former CPR station at left.

The line was built by the Ontario and Quebec Railway (O&Q), which had been incorporated in 1871 when just about everybody was getting in on the railway craze. For a decade the O&Q was a railway company in name only, and it wasn't until its charter was acquired in 1881 that any construction was undertaken. Not surprisingly, the principals involved in the takeover were members of a syndicate controlling the CPR, a fast-growing railway that was desperately seeking access to the lucrative Toronto market, which until then had been monopolized by the Grand Trunk Railway. The goal of the O&Q was to quickly build a line joining Toronto with Perth, where trains could access existing CPR tracks that connected Perth with Ottawa and Montreal, the new country's largest and most important city.

A pre-TTC wooden streetcar rumbles by the CPR's soon-to-open $250,000 North Toronto Station. Unfortunately, the photographer lopped off the tower so we'll never know what time the picture was taken.

To accomplish its goal — the all-important Toronto connection — a line would be laid through part of rural York Township to the north of Toronto. The line would connect the O&Q tracks recently laid from Perth west to Agincourt with the tracks of the busy Credit Valley and Toronto, Grey and Bruce railways at West Toronto Junction. Both railways, which would become part of the O&Q by the end of 1883, ran over a common right-of-way from the Junction (a name resulting from the junction of these two pioneer rail lines) to the old Union Station on the city's waterfront. With the completion of the line between Agincourt and West Toronto, the O&Q attained its goal. It came as no surprise when, on January 4, 1884, the O&Q was leased by the CPR for 999 years.

Thus it is that the former O&Q rail line that heads east out of West Toronto, parallels Dupont Street, crosses Bathurst Street,

Avenue Road, Yonge Street, and Mt. Pleasant Road, then heads northeaster through Leaside (another old railway town), under the Bayview Extension, over Don Mills Road, and the Don Valley Parkway, and so on, is now part of the CPR.

CPR's Yonge Street Station timetable for the year 1923.

One of the main features of this line is the former North Toronto railway station on the east side of Yonge Street between St. Clair Avenue and Davenport Road. Though opened in 1916 to serve rail passenger traffic, the building has spent most of its life as a government store: it opened as LCBO Store # 10 in 1940.

Toronto Sketches 6

While it's true the station replaced a small station that stood for years west of Yonge Street, the real reason for such a magnificent station has more to do with our present Union Station, or should I say, the lack of it.

The idea of a modern, new Union Station to serve the travelling needs of Toronto's nearly 200 000 citizens dates to the early years of this century. In fact, to a time almost coincident with the extinguishing of the 1904 conflagration that scoured a site that had long been proposed as the location of a new station. Finally, after years of quarrelling amongst all levels of government and the two major railways, the Canadian Pacific and the Grand Trunk (thus the term *union*), an exasperated CPR decided to erect its own station. The time was right for another reason. The increase in vehicle traffic made the level crossings extremely dangerous, so a major grade separation program across the top of the city (which would necessitate a replacement station) was undertaken.

The new CPR North Toronto Station opened on June 14, 1915, and for a time it, too, was a union station, with another national transcontinental railway, Sir William Mackenzie's ill-fated Canadian Northern Railway (CNoR), a short-term occupant. Just one year after the station opened on June 14, 1916, the CNoR vanished, becoming part of the mix of railways that would emerge in 1923 as the CNR.

It was obvious to many that with the long-awaited opening of the new Union Station in August of 1927 the CPR's abandonment of its North Toronto Station was not far off. In fact, by the end of 1930 the last trains, those serving Montreal and Owen Sound, were no longer using the station, having been re-routed to the new station on Front Street.

Over the years there have been all sorts of redevelopment schemes for the property, including a 1970 proposal that would have seen the station and its landmark tower demolished and a 19-acre complex of apartment towers and a two-level shopping mall constructed on the site with the tracks placed in a half-mile-long tunnel.

AIRPORT MEMORIES TAKE FLIGHT

August 23, 1998

In the background is Malton Airport's new terminal building, which opened in 1949. At the time it was described as "the Empire's finest." Incidentally, the car in the view is a 1955 Pontiac, just like mine. I wonder...

A couple of weeks ago I was lucky enough to be invited by organizer Brian Willer to a reunion of former Victory Aircraft employees that took place in the Boeing Aircraft plant adjacent to Pearson International Airport. Though the name Victory Aircraft is just a vague memory to the older generation and usually draws a complete blank when mentioned to the younger set, there was a time during the darkest days of the Second World War when the products from factories such as Victory were virtually all that stood between eventual freedom and Axis world domination.

More than 100 former Victory Aircraft workers showed up that rainy afternoon, and the stories, like the mighty Lancaster bombers these ladies and gentlemen assembled from 1942 to 1945, flew fast and wide. Some of the guests had brought mementos of their days at Victory, including a nicely framed set of wrenches, programs and pictures of company social events and a pair of work overalls complete with the distinctive Victoria Aircraft Limited logo.

All present eagerly waited for the weather to clear so that one of only two flying Lancasters in the world, the famed Mynarski Lancaster from the Canadian Warplane Heritage Museum near Hamilton, could put in an appearance. The plan was to have it do a flypast then taxi up to the building where it was born in July 1945, and where its creators could give it a big and loving welcome home.

Unfortunately, the weather did not co-operate, and the Lancaster appearance had to be scrubbed. As disappointing as that was, the group partied on and everyone had a good time, most vowing to do again next year.

As I left the hangar to return to my car in a far-off parking lot, I noticed well in the distance a strange-looking aircraft taxiing to the end of runway 06L/24R readying for takeoff. Closer inspection revealed that it was one of British Airways' fabulous Concordes. (A subsequent conversation with British Airways confirmed that the Concorde wasn't a regular visitor to our city. This particular aircraft was picking up passengers for a special charter flight over the North Pole.)

I stood spellbound as the mighty aircraft swept down the nearby rain-soaked runway, engines roaring, thin pencils of flame shooting out of the exhaust pipes. Suddenly it lifted into the air, quickly boring a tunnel in the low flying clouds, into which it disappeared. Only the incredible sound of its engines continued, then that too was gone. Wow!

Interestingly, when I was preparing this week's column on the Victory Aircraft reunion, it came to me that the arrival of that Concorde was within a few weeks of the 60th anniversary of the arrival of the very first plane to land at was known way back then as Malton Airport, a geographical reference to the nearby farm community, pretty much the only thing for miles around.

On that warm, sunny day, August 29, 1938 (60 years ago next Saturday, if anyone is looking to party), an American Airlines DC-3 carrying officials of the airline, a few Toronto politicians, and representatives of Chicago, Detroit, and local newspapers to that year's CNE, became the newly constructed airport's first patron. Of course, the event was covered with great gusto in the daily papers, most reporting that the visiting plane "rocketed" to Toronto at "more than 3 miles a minute." Before the company flagship proceeded to the new airport it passed over the heads of the

Today's Lester B. Pearson International Airport. A portion of Highway 401 is at the top left of the photo, Highway 427 crosses at the bottom, and Highway 409 hooks into the airport at the right. Airport Terminals 2, 1, and 3 (left to right) are at the centre (photo courtesy GTAA).

Exhibition crowd who were able to hear, through the CNE public address system, greetings being sent their way by various members on board the goodwill flight high overhead. CBC carried the same comments to radio listeners coast to coast.

To say that Malton Airport, a name that was changed to Toronto International, then Pearson International in 1960 and 1984 respectively, has grown in size over the past six decades is very much an understatement. In the beginning the control tower and passenger waiting facilities were jammed into a former farmhouse. Today, there is a trio of terminals to serve airport users who in 1997 numbered more than 26 million. In 1938 the new airport, which covered a little over 1 000 acres and had two paved runways, was designed, built, and operated by the Toronto Harbour Commission. In 1996 the facility — which now covers nearly 4 500 acres, has four runways (the longest more than 11 000 feet in length) and serves 61 different airlines — became the responsibility of the newly created Greater Toronto Airports Authority. And more spectacular changes are on the way.

IT'S THE WHEEL THING AT THE CNE

August 30, 1998

For the first time in many, many years, the Automotive Building down at the Ex is being used for exactly what it was built for, cars. During this year's Ex the magnificent old building will be home to an exhibit titled "Car of the Century," a selection of 100 unique vehicles selected by a number judges from all over the world. The selection seems to be weighted in favour of European models, but perhaps I'm just sore 'cause my 1955 Pontiac was not included.

The CNE's beautiful new Automotive Building hosted its first Auto Show in 1929.

To be sure, over the years there have been numerous specialty car shows put on in the building. However, the last time that it was filled with cars during the annual Exhibition was way back in 1967. Historically, the reason the traditional CNE car show lost favour had more to do with the dates of the fair than anything else. That's because the fair was originally held later in the summer, from the end of August well into September. This allowed the next year's models to be unveiled during the Exhibition. In fact, it was during the 1954 Ex that the public first saw the 1955 Ford Thunderbird. Canadians even got to see Preston Tucker's revolutionary "tin goose" at the Ex just a few months after its world premier south of the border on June 19, 1947.

One of the most spectacular car shows ever held at the Ex must have been the 1953 version, when General Motors used the opportunity to present "Dreams on Wheels," during which fair goers were able to view "the world's most advanced cars." There was the brand new Corvette by Chevrolet, "now in limited production," the brochure announced. Nearby were the "dazzling" Oldsmobile Starfire, the "glamorous" Pontiac Parisienne, the "spectacular" Cadillac Le Mans, and Buick's XP-300, "as streamlined as tomorrow's jets."

Described as being "as streamlined as tomorrow's jets," the Buick XP-300 was front and centre at the 1953 CNE Car Show held in the Automotive Building.

In the same building, over in the corner, was something called a Volkswagen. This was the its first appearance at a CNE car show. "Drop by and see why the VW is the most sought after car in Europe today." By the way, the cost of the car was $1 595, a figure that included heater, defroster, turn signals and double windshield wipers.

As popular as the car shows had become, by the mid-1960s the show's future was in doubt. This was because CNE officials had decided to move opening day earlier into August. This was done in deference to the farmers who, while displaying their produce at the fair, were more interested in getting back to their farms. Another problem officials were trying to resolve was the exodus of hundreds of student workers once school opened.

One negative result of this change in dates was the fact that the only cars available for display in the Automotive Building were, for all intents and purposes, the previous year's models. Obviously, neither the manufacturers nor the dealerships found the situation acceptable, and it wasn't long before the long-time tradition of the new car show at the Ex died.

Just how long this tradition had gone on is clouded in the mists of time, but we do know that in 1904 (when the CNE was still called the Toronto Industrial Exhibition), a few pioneer car manufacturers rented space in buildings or under tents at the fair to show off the new horseless carriages. So great was the interest in these new machines, a few years later officials decided to erect a special structure just to house the automobile displays. But, because boat and airplane manufacturers also wanted access to the fair goers, the new structure, which opened in 1908, was given the more generic name of Transportation Building. Visitors to the 1974 edition of the CNE will recall that the old building featured a Spanish exhibit. During the fair the structure burned to the ground.

Returning to the CNE's Automotive Building for a moment, this lovely structure, which officials dubbed the Automobile Salon, a name that didn't catch on, was erected at a cost of $1 million, with the money provided by the automotive industry and the Canadian National Exhibition. Newspaper accounts of the official opening on August 26, 1929, declared that the building, which was designed by Canadian architect Douglas Kertland and built almost exclusively out of Canadian materials by Canadian labour, was the "largest and finest building on the American continent devoted exclusively to the showing of cars."

It's fitting that this year we have fine old cars in a fine old building. Go see both.

FAREWELL TO A CNE LANDMARK

September 6, 1998

I f you're planning to visit the Ex today or tomorrow be sure to take along your camera. Why? This will be the last time you'll be able to get a picture of the CNE Grandstand complete with throngs of fair goers. It has been decreed that sometime in October the mammoth structure will go the way of several other old Exhibition buildings — the Art Gallery, the Electrical and Engineering Building, the International Building, and more recently, the Shell Tower.

The 1906 grandstand served well until destroyed by fire in 1946. Note the helmeted Toronto policeman in the foreground.

To be sure, there have been all kinds of reasons put forward suggesting that the Grandstand be retained. The most compelling has to do with the possibility of Toronto being awarded the 2008 Olympics. If that comes to pass, a fixed-up Grandstand would without question be a useful venue for certain events. However, with few exceptions (such as the retention of old City Hall and Union Station, both of which remain standing thanks mainly to a determined citizenry), such forward thinking has never been a particularly strong attribute of those in charge. Let's hope our elected officials do better as they duke it out over the future of Heritage Toronto, a board set up to advise politicians on the future of our past.

According to information gathered by Linda Cobon, the CNE archivist, today's Grandstand is the fourth in the Ex's long history. The first was a 5 000-seat wooden structure that was used from the first Toronto Industrial Exhibition (the CNE's original name) in the fall of 1879 until it was replaced by a larger grandstand with twice the seating capacity 16 years later. Both facilities accommodated spectators for harness racing, livestock judging, fireworks displays and, starting in 1884, elaborate and usually patriotic stage shows.

The immense size of the four-year-old CNE grandstand is obvious in this 1951 aerial photo.

Early in 1906 the Ex was visited by a ferocious fire that destroyed the Crystal Palace — the fair's main exhibit building — as well as the nearby grandstand. Later that year workers completed construction of a replacement grandstand. It was located to the southeast of the previous one and had seating for more than 16 000 spectators. this grandstand would be a fixture at the Ex for the next four decades. As an aside, two years after the fire the present Horticultural Building opened on the site of the fire-ravaged Crystal Palace.

War was declared in 1939, and it wasn't long before city and fair officials were discussing how they could help in the war effort. As things in Europe went from bad to worse it became obvious that the training of troops was more important than the holding of an annual exhibition. As a result it was decided to cancel the 1942 CNE and turn the grounds into a military encampment, to be known as Manning Depot No. 1.

Hostilities ended in 1945, but it was too late to organize a fair for that year. Instead, plans went ahead for the 1946 edition, but before the gates would open a fire in April of that year once again destroyed the grandstand.

Work began immediately on its replacement. And this time it would be indestructible. Toronto architects Marani and Morris designed an 800-foot-long, 75-foot-high steel and reinforced concrete structure faced with Queenston limestone and red brick. Even its roof would be an engineering marvel through the use of steel cantilevered trusses that permitted an unobstructed view from almost every one of its 22 000 seats. Two large dining halls and a 15 000-square-foot exhibit hall would be incorporated into the space under the seating area. Visitors to the 1948 CNE jammed the new structure to watch Jack Kochman and his Champion Hell Drivers (sort of an early version of rush hour on the 401) and "those Atom-o-Comical, Jest-Propelled Fun-Bombs" Olsen and Johnson in their famous *Laffcade of 1948* with "a cast of 150 including a chorus of 72 plus 48 dazzling beauties."

The new grandstand received accolades from admirers far and wide.

In 1959 portable bleachers for 12 472 were erected on the south side of the field, following which the CFL Toronto Argos moved to the CNE from Varsity Stadium. In 1976, after the bleachers were demolished, new permanent seating was added, bringing the capacity of CNE Stadium to 54 264. Finally, Toronto had a big-league facility, albeit a retrofitted grandstand. With the necessary facility we were awarded a major-league franchise. No way was it a "mistake by the lake." On April 7, 1977, the Blue Jays played their first regular game at the CNE grandstand stadium, defeating Chicago White Sox (in the snow) 9 to 5. A dozen years later both the Jays and the Argos moved to the new SkyDome.

The CNE grandstand's fate was sealed.

MAJOR MACKENZIE'S HOME NOW PART OF PIONEER PAST

September 13, 1998

N ow that another busy summer is almost history it's time that I do some catching up. Over the past few months readers have sent in letters requesting answers to questions. A particularly interesting query arrived in the mail several weeks ago. It had to do with the origin of the name Major Mackenzie Drive, an exit familiar to travellers using Highway 400. It's the one in the general vicinity of Canada's Wonderland. In fact, it was during my three-year stint working at the park (I had been hired during the construction phase by Taft Broadcasting, the American developer, because of my "Canadian accent") that I first became interested in the derivation of the name of this particular road. Many will recall that years ago it was called the Maple Side Road.

Major Mackenzie of Major Mackenzie Drive fame.

The reader may wonder whether the name had anything to do with William Lyon Mackenzie, Toronto's first mayor and the guy who tried to overthrow the government back in 1837. While the surnames are spelled the same, the Mackenzie in question is in reality the late

Major Alexander Mackenzie, a long-time resident of Woodbridge, Ontario, who was born in 1886 in a small log house on the family farm. "Lex," as he was known for most of his 85 years, was schooled in Woodbridge, after which he became a successful farmer. He served his country during the Great War, where he proved to be a gallant soldier. Mackenzie was wounded at Vimy Ridge, elevated to the rank of major on the battlefields of France, and awarded the Military Cross.

After the war he returned to his farm and years later entered the wonderful world of politics. He served as the area provincial member of parliament from 1945 until his retirement in 1967. Major Mackenzie died in 1970.

As for Mackenzie's log house, which stood near a pair of dusty crossroads since 1830, it eventually found itself dangerously close to what had evolved into the busy intersection of Highway 7 and Islington Avenue. To preserve the historic structure for future generations, it was moved to Black Creek Pioneer Village, where it can still be seen and toured.

The ancient Mackenzie homestead, once located just outside the village of Woodbridge, is now safe and sound in Black Creek Pioneer Village.

**I'm frequently asked which books are the most useful when researching the history of Toronto and area. Without question the Bible of Toronto reference books is a six-volume set titled *Landmarks of Toronto*, the creation of *Telegram* publisher and Toronto history expert John Ross Robertson. The set sells for about $1 000, but you can browse through it at several public libraries. *Landmarks of*

Toronto is a compilation of columns on numerous aspects of the city's history, which appeared in the old Toronto *Evening Telegram* newspaper between 1894 and 1914. One key ingredient that makes these columns and the book so entertaining and informative was the hundreds of sketches of people, buildings, street scenes, and skylines drawn by *Telegram* staff artist Owen Staples. Now, thanks to the efforts of Staples's grandson Rod Staples, the life of Owen Staples has finally been documented in a book titled *Owen Staples, Painter of Canada's Past.*

A PALATIAL SCHEME WITHOUT PIER

September 20, 1998

Only a few hundred feet of the mile-and-a-third-long million-dollar pier ever got built.
Where'd the money go? No one's talking. In the background, the bridges over the
Humber River continue to be replaced with a more modern structure.

Seventy years ago the citizens of Toronto were being told of a new development that would alter the look of the city's western waterfront. The project would be known as the Palace Pier and would be larger and, at $1.25 million, far more costly than its namesake attraction in Brighton, England.

The new Palace Pier would consist of four structures, including a 30 000-square-foot dance hall, a huge palace of fun, a bandstand, and a 1 400-seat theatre, all sitting astride a gaily illuminated pier stretching from the west side of the mouth of the Humber River nearly a third of a mile out into Lake Ontario. There would even be provisions for lake steamers from near and far to tie up along the pier wall, allowing thousands easy access to this "guaranteed money maker."

At least that's how the promoters described the project in a prospectus as they eagerly sold $10 shares in this "can't lose" proposition. Money flowed in, but for reasons now shrouded in time, only a few hundred feet of pier were ever built. And even when this part of the project was completed, the abbreviated pier stood empty for years. Finally, on June 23, 1941, the new Strathcona Palace Pier roller skating rink opened to the public. Several days later radio and movie star Bob Hope, who was in town promoting *Caught in the Draft*, his latest film, christened the new Palace Pier by doing a few laps around the shiny hardwood floor.

Way back in 1945 fans flocked to the Palace Pier to welcome home the Leaf team that had just won the Stanley Cup in Detroit. Memories...

Bandleader Jimmy Dorsey played the Palace Pier in 1945.

Perennial favourite Bob Hope helped open the struggling Palace Pier during a promotional visit in 1941.

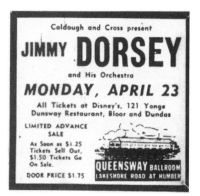

Many readers will remember the Palace Pier as a popular dance hall, but the big bands didn't move in until 1943. By then the place had been renamed the Queensway Ballroom, a name that was eventually changed back to the original Palace Pier. The popular Trump Davidson was the best known of the Canadian bandleaders to play the Pier.

Over the years the building served a variety of purposes until it was set afire one cold night in early January, 1963. The following morning, the memory-filled Toronto landmark was just ashes. Two condominium towers now stand on the site.

Behind the towers, at the foot of nearby Palace Pier Court, is a portion of one the old pier's original footings surrounded by several old photos of one of the city's most popular attractions.

THE HOUSES THAT BISHOP BUILT

September 27, 1998

T he Guinness Book of World Records reveals that the oldest capital city in the world is Damascus, Syria, which has been continuously inhabited since c. 2500 B.C. Rome dates back to 753 B.C., and London, England, to 400 B.C. Toronto, on the other hand, is a relative newcomer as world communities go, having been established by Europeans as recently as 1793. Often, as I conduct my various walking tours, overseas visitors comment on just how young we are and how new all our buildings are, even our old ones. For obvious reasons it's difficult for them to get excited over what we regard as our historic structures.

One of the oldest structures in Toronto, the 1842 Paul Bishop Houses are part of the building that still occupies the southeast corner of Adelaide and Sherbourne streets.

Nevertheless, many of us worship places such as Montgomery's Inn in Etobicoke (1830), Old City Hall (1899), the Princes' Gates (1927), and even the Bank of Commerce that opened in the early 1930s on King Street just west of Yonge. Not ancient, perhaps, but not bad for a place that's just a little more that a couple of centuries old.

With so few ancient monuments still in existence, it's no wonder that the various historical and architectural societies around town, as well as Heritage Toronto and the other municipal historical boards, make a great to-do when something really old (at least in the way we define *really old*) becomes threatened. Alarm bells become even louder when that structure sits within the original Town of York, a ten-block area bounded by today's George, Adelaide (then Duke), Berkeley (Parliament), and Front (Palace) streets, a site that was the genesis of today's sprawling Toronto, former suburbs and all.

When a major residential project for the block bounded by Sherbourne, Adelaide, Princess, and King was announced recently, the old building complex situated at the southeast corner of Sherbourne and Adelaide streets was threatened, and those bells went off. Known as the Paul Bishop Houses, the structure, while much altered over the years, retains portions of buildings that are among the oldest in the city and probably the only residential structures we have that survived the Great Fire of 1849 that ravaged much of this part of the young city.

To be sure we still have a few commercial buildings of the same vintage in the old city, several of which have been restored and are now well looked after. These include the Bank of Upper Canada and First Toronto Post Office, 252 and 260 Adelaide Street East, and Toronto's Second City Hall (incorporated into the South St. Lawrence Market). Indicative of the compactness of the city back then just blocks away are residences known as the Paul Bishop Houses.

Bishop is described in Volume 1 of Robertson's Landmarks of Toronto, the undisputed Bible of Torontoniana, as "an early settler [who was] a French Canadian [and] whose real name L'Eveque — the bishop— was Anglicized when he moved to Upper Canada [Ontario]." He was proficient in a number of trades — blacksmith, mechanic, and pattern maker, to name just a few — and holds the distinction of building the province's first cab, obviously a horse-drawn contraption.

Further reading reveals that Bishop's workshop was on the northeast corner of Sherbourne and Adelaide, and it was here that pioneer cab man Thornton Blackburn's cab was built in 1837. Research by staff at Heritage Toronto has determined that five years later Bishop moved across the street to reside in a newly constructed brick house. Unfortunately, Bishop suffered business setbacks that forced him to move away from Toronto.

As the years passed, the building was altered and not in a particularly sympathetic manner. It became home to a variety of commercial and industrial concerns and now sits unoccupied. Close examination, however, will reveal traces of the 1842 structures. In fact, the developers of the new project for the site plan to incorporate the "ancient monument" in their development. For what purpose, I don't know. But stay tuned.

Sketch of the Paul Bishop Houses, southeast corner of Caroline (now Sherbourne) and Duke (now Adelaide) streets, c 1842, from *Landmarks of Toronto*.

STREET STANDS FRONT AND CENTRE

October 4, 1998

As regular readers of this column will know, one of my fascinations with our city's rich history is discovering the origins of the names of its various streets. While the reasons for some choices are impossible to determine (on occasion the names of family pets or a favourite author have been used), more often than not the choice was based on some historical event, prominent citizen, or birthplace of a pioneer settler. In the case of Front Street, however, the reason for the name's selection was even simpler. The thoroughfare, one of the first to be laid out, was — are you ready for this? — the front street of the young community. If you walked any farther south your hat would start to float.

The open-sided streetcar approaching the corner of Front and Bay tells us it's summertime in Toronto. The year is 1912, and in the centre background is the popular Queen's Hotel.

To be historically accurate, there was a time when officials attempted to have the stretch of the cross-waterfront thoroughfare east of the market called by a more grandiose title, Palace Street. This was because it led to the original Palace of Parliament, a couple of rudimentary brick buildings erected near the water's edge at the east end of town that were used as the original seat of the provincial government in Toronto (then still called York). These structures were the forerunner of our present Parliament Buildings at the top of University Avenue. Incidentally, it was the location of these buildings that resulted in the naming of the street that led to and from them, Parliament Street.

Same view, 1998. The Royal York Hotel now towers over the scene.

As the town (a city after 1834) began to develop, the unpleasantness of the Don River forced the sprawl to take place in a westerly direction. As this expansion continued, so too did the lengthening of Front Street (by now the term Palace had been dropped) all the way to the Second Concession west of Yonge, a simple dirt path that was originally known as Crookshank's Lane, as it led to the Hon. George Crookshank's rural cottage near the present Dundas Street corner. Later it was renamed Bathurst in honour of Earl Bathurst, Secretary of the Colonies in British North America. (Gee, all these names — must be a book in there somewhere).

About 1843 brick row houses, known collectively as the Ontario Terrace, were erected on the north side of Front Street overlooking Tinning's Wharf, the bay, and directly opposite what would eventually become the site of the city's majestic new Union Station. Three years later the houses were remodelled and became the new home of Knox College. In 1853 the houses were converted once again, this time for hotel purposes. First it was Sword's Hotel, then the Revere House, and finally the Queen's Hotel. From the latter's inception in 1862 until its demolition in 1927, to make way for the new Royal York Hotel, it was known far and wide as the finest hotel in the province, if not in the entire country.

** Last week (September 27, 1998) I wrote about the Paul Bishop Houses at the southeast corner of Sherbourne and Adelaide streets, one of the oldest building complexes remaining in the city. The people at Heritage Toronto tell me that the structure, which predates the Great Fire of 1849, during which many of the young community's original structures were burnt to the ground, has a new lease on life. It is to be incorporated into a new residential development planned for the site.

This interest in what few buildings still stand in the old part of the city is thanks in great measure to a relatively new organization called Citizens for the Old Town. You can learn more about this group and its interests by contacting the organization c/o Toronto's First Post Office, 260 Adelaide Street East, Toronto, Ontario M5A 1N1.

1915 FIT FORD TO A "T"

October 11, 1998

The former Ford automobile factory at Dupont and Christie streets is now home to a number of businesses.

As the days get shorter and the temperature begins to drop, those of us lucky enough to own a classic automobile will soon have to think about putting it away for another year. With a final wash, a trip to the gas station to top up the tank, a little extra air in the tires, and a dozen other things, that'll be it until the warm breezes in May (April with any luck) announce that the time's right to let the old-timer out of the garage for another summer of fun.

Having visited and even participated in a number of cruise nights over the past few months (a cruise night is where dozens and dozens of makes and models of old cars are put on show for the benefit of other collectors and the general public — but please don't touch), my favourite classic (not counting my own 1955 Pontiac) is the Model T Ford. Having said that, I realize that I run the risk of being censured by my car collecting colleagues. However, if I don't make that Model T assumption, the subject of this week's column just won't fit.

The first of Henry Ford's Ts appeared in 1908. The revolutionary car was easy to mass produce, easy to repair, and with its wooden body mounted on a steel frame was described as being "stronger than a horse and easier to maintain." It also had something else going for it. At something around $800, just about anyone could afford to buy one of Henry's cars.

The first Ford vehicle built in Canada was the Model C. It was produced at the company's Walkerville plant in 1905, the year after

Ford of Canada was incorporated. Walkerville would amalgamate with the city of Windsor in 1935.

MADE IN CANADA

The 1917 Ford Touring Car

THE old reliable Ford Chassis---stream line effect---crown fenders---tapered hood---new radiator with increased cooling surface.

Chassis . .	$450	Coupelet . .	$695
Runabout . .	475	Town Car ,	780
Touring Car .	495	Sedan . . .	890

f.o.b. Ford, Ontario

Ford Motor Company of Canada
Limited

Toronto Branch, corner Christie and Dupont Sts.

Assembly and Service Branches at St. John, N.B.; Montreal, Que.; Toronto, Ont.; Hamilton, Ont.; London, Ont.; Winnipeg, Man.; Saskatoon, Sask.; Calgary, Alta.; Vancouver, B.C.

Ad for Model T Fords that were assembled in Ford's Toronto factory at Christie and Dupont streets from 1915 to 1923.

Following the success of the new Model T, company officials began examining various ways of increasing production. One idea they hit upon was to ship packing crates full of engines, drivetrains, transmissions, and hundreds of other bits and pieces to newly erected factories in major centres around the world. There, workers would unpack the crates, lay out the parts, and begin assembling new Model Ts.

Toronto was an ideal site for a factory, and the site chosen for the new plant was at the northwest corner of Dupont and Christie streets, a location handy for workers living in the nearby neighborhood and adjacent to the CPR track over which trainloads of crates would arrive daily from the main Walkerville factory. The building still stands and until recently was the home of not wheel nuts, but Planter's Peanuts.

Ford's new Toronto home opened the week of February 22, 1915, which just happened to coincide with that year's car show, an annual event put on by the city's various car dealers. This show was the forerunner of the present Canadian International Auto Show that's also held in February at the Toronto Convention Centre.

Thanks to an ancient newspaper article I recently found I'm able to take you on a tour of the building. Here on the main floor is a richly appointed showroom, a customer waiting room, the general and executive offices, a lunchroom for the female workers and, at the rear, a modern garage. On the second floor are the loading and unloading facilities for the crates that continually arrived by boxcar from the main plant. Here too is a huge parts stockroom and across the hall a second room in which busy salesmen could rest themselves and their busy pencils. The entire third floor is a repair shop complete with the most up-to-date tools and equipment. The assembly line is located one floor above, and this is where the parts in those crates are turned into nice, shiny Model Ts. On the fifth floor is the paint shop, where customers could have their vehicle finished in any colour, as long as that colour was black. Now we're on the roof, where each new product is put through its paces on an a much abbreviated version of a full-size test track.

The building remained as a Ford Model T factory until 1923 when the company moved to larger facilities, a building that's now part of Shoppers World at the southwest corner of Danforth and Victoria Park avenues. The Model T continued in production here until replaced by the Model A in 1928. Ford left Toronto altogether when the Oakville plant opened in 1953.

Meanwhile, back at the Christie and Dupont building, Mr. Planters' peanuts eventually replaced the wheel and engine block nuts, and today it's the site of a Blockbuster video outlet.

**Formerly known as Toronto Township, the Town of Mississauga came into being at midnight, December 31, 1967. Seven years later the town amalgamated with nearby Port Credit and Streetsville, and the City of Mississauga was born. As young as our neighbour to the west may be, it too has a fascinating history much of which is presented in the Bradley Museum — an 1830s farmhouse described as a piece of the country in the heart of the city — and Benares Historic House. Beautiful Benares, considered by many to be the inspiration for the world-famous Jalna series, has been lovingly restored by the Ontario Heritage Foundation to the way it would have appeared in 1918. Call (905) 822-1569 for addresses and operating times.

MYSTERY PHOTO IS AN HISTORICAL GEM

October 18, 1998

One of the benefits of writing a weekly column is the feedback I get from my readers. While all letters are welcome, my eyes really light up when an envelope arrives containing something more than a letter. A case in point is a bulkier than normal envelope that arrived a couple of weeks ago from a reader in Oshawa. She had recently gone through some family possessions and rather than throwing what appeared to be simply an old photo into the closest trash bin, she decided to send them to me, just in case I'd find it of interest.

Souvenir commemorative photo showing Yonge Street south of the present College–Carlton intersection just before the arrival of the returning troops on July 23, 1885.

The photo was of some street, somewhere, a bit of a mystery at first although the photographer's name along the border, Mickelthwaite, suggested it was, in fact, a Toronto street scene. And while I didn't know where it was taken, the names Batoche, Fish Creek, and Cut Knife on the evergreen-covered arch plus the statement Honour To Our Heroes soon made it obvious that the event depicted was the return in 1885 of government troops from the Saskatchewan district in the Northwest Territories where they had been sent to subdue the Métis leader Louis Riel. Those place names were the sites of battles fought between troops of the young Dominion of Canada and the Métis, Plains Indians, and a few white settlers.

A closer look revealed that the soldiers depicted in the paintings on either side of what was known as a triumphal arch (a common celebration piece back then) were members of two Toronto regiments, the Queen's Own Rifles and the 10th Royal Grenadiers (since 1936 the Royal Regiment of Canada). This fact confirmed that the location in the view was indeed somewhere in our city. But where? The search was on.

Examining a city directory of 1885 and using the presence of streetcar tracks, names on the signs in front of a few of the buildings (Pearsall, Dominion Brush), and the street address #402 to the extreme right of the view, I was able to deduce that the photo was taken looking south on Yonge from just below the present-day College–Carlton intersection. The street to the left of the arch was McGill, and to the right, old Buchanan Street, which was obliterated when Eaton's College Street store (now College Park) was built 45 years after the photo was taken.

Subsequent examination of the *Evening Telegram* newspaper in the *Sun* News Research Centre soon revealed that the troops arrived at the old North Toronto railway station at 4:00 p.m. on July 23, 1885, and marched down Yonge Street to the City Hall of the day at Front and Jarvis streets, where they were welcomed by Lieutenant Governor Robinson, Mayor Manning, and city council, plus hundreds and hundreds of wildly cheering citizens. This picture was taken while some of those citizens waited for their heroes to march under the arch south of the Yonge and College–Carlton corner.

Case solved!

CITY'S PAST VANISHES WITH ARRIVAL OF NEW BUILDINGS

October 25, 1998

During that period in Toronto's history when the city eagerly sought to have its name added to the list of so-called "world-class cities," many of its fine old buildings were ruthlessly sacrificed. Sure, a few citizens attempted to entice the city fathers of the day to be more circumspect about which buildings would vanish in the name of progress and which would remain to reflect Toronto's past. Most notable amongst those eager to preserve the best of our built heritage was Professor Eric Arthur, the author of *No Mean City* (U of T Press, 1964, revised in 1986 by Stephen Otto). This book continues to be a Bible of Toronto's architectural history.

More than three decades have gone by since Professor Arthur's book first arrived on city bookstore shelves, and it's interesting to review that 1964 edition to see what marvellous buildings we have lost in spite of the professor's wise counselling that a great city doesn't consist entirely of shiny new buildings. Gone now are the Eighth Post Office, which stood at the top of Toronto Street, the Mental Asylum on Queen Street West, and the I.O.F.'s Temple Building, northwest corner of Bay and Adelaide streets.

Though the building is listed in the book, the fate of the Armouries on University Avenue had been sealed months before the book's appearance. The Armouries was a rambling building with a castle-like facade that stood on the east side of the street just south of the aptly named Armoury Street, a street name that accurately reflected the structure's original name when it opened in 1895.

Interestingly, the genesis of the University Avenue Armouries (I'll stick to the name by which it was known when the end finally came) was the North West Rebellion of 1885, mentioned in last week's column. In those days the building that served as an armouries was the old Drill Shed behind the City Hall of the day, at the southwest corner of Front and Jarvis streets. The south end of the South St. Lawrence Market stands on the site today.

This ramshackle facility was less than satisfactory (one winter the roof collapsed after a heavy snowfall), and the city fathers frequently petitioned the federal government for a new building, one that would better reflect the city's loyalty to the Dominion of Canada and its willingness to defend the young nation's future come what may.

The roof is off as workers begin demolition of the University Avenue Armouries in the early fall of 1963. New City Hall is taking shape in the top right background.

By March 1886 all concerned had finally agreed on a new building that would combine a drill hall, a drill ground, and an armoury, the latter term referring to a secure storage space for munitions and weapons. The new building would be erected on a piece of property at the west end of the city on Peter Street. But there was a slight problem. The influential property owner refused the price offered by the government, and soon the hunt for a site was back on.

Some on the committee wanted the armoury built on Richmond Street, west of Peter. Not surprisingly, the residents of the area didn't. More searching, and finally the University Avenue (still known as University Street) location, which in the late 1880s was still residential in nature, was agreed upon. This time opposition voiced by the residents of the half dozen or so small houses in peril fell on deaf ears. By July, 1890, the deal to acquire the property had been completed at a cost of $125 000. Exactly one year later construction of Toronto's new Armoury began.

Officially opened in 1895, the Armoury became a focal point as hundreds of young Toronto men came forward to sign up so they could assist Great Britain in her dispute with the Boers in South

Africa. And again during the Great War, the Second World War, and the Korean conflict, it was within the sturdy walls of the University Avenue Armouries (the name was now pluralized) that more than a quarter of a million young Canadian men and women answered the call to defend the nation, the Commonwealth, and the entire free world from the ravages of tyranny. Sadly, many of those who took the colours at the Armouries would never return to enjoy the freedom for which they so valiantly fought.

By 1956, war memories were quickly fading into the past. Word got out that plans were being discussed that would see the Armouries demolished and a courthouse erected on the site to serve the needs of the new Municipality of Metropolitan Toronto (remember that place?).

At first there was some confusion as to who actually owned the property, the federal government or the city. While the discussions went on, and perhaps to preclude another disaster as nearly happened at the old Drill Shed a century before, a new roof was put on the Armouries.

Talks continued, and eventually it was determined that the federal government owned both the site and the structure. Both were soon sold to the new Metro corporation for $2 million. The deal complete, Metro officials quickly announced that the old building would be torn down and a courthouse erected in its place as soon as feasible.

That decision ignited a controversy that pitted war veterans of all ages against most of the politicians. One notable exception was perennial city councillor Allan Lamport, and though he drew several fellow politicians to his side, it was too little, too late. And while the controversy lasted for more than three years, the arrival of teams of wrecking crews in August, 1963, finally ended the battle.

Had that battle erupted in recent years, would the Armouries still be with us? With our more enlightened view of our city's past, I'd like to think so. But who knows.

FILLING USED TO BE A JOY AT THE PUMPS

November 1, 1998

It constantly amazes me how many of today's news stories reflect news stories of yesterday. A good example of this is the ongoing question as to whether the public is really being gouged by the big oil companies, or is it all a series of coincidences?. Do they really raise prices in order to take advantage of the thousands who take to the highways on long weekends? And why is it that when one station raises its prices, everyone else in town follows at almost the same instance? And do the large companies force the smaller guys out of business by manipulating wholesale prices?

While I certainly don't have any answers to these questions, I do know that these same queries have been going on for decades. In fact, there's little doubt that when the pump price at Canada's first gasoline station on Cambie Street in Vancouver jumped from 20¢ to 21¢ a gallon people cried out, "We're being had!" or whatever the expression was back in 1907.

The years went by and in 1938 ads began appearing advising Toronto motorists that the Joy Oil Company would protect them from the oil trust "witches" who controlled gasoline prices throughout the city. The story of this upstart company, whose 14 Toronto gas stations looked like miniature French chateaus, is as fascinating as it is short.

Incorporated in Canada in 1936 by Margaret Austin, the wife of Charles Austin, who together owned Detroit's Sunny Service Oil Company, the new Joy Oil Company Ltd. was in trouble with Toronto city council right from the start. Unable to get permission to erect storage tanks on the waterfront, although other, larger companies had, Margaret Austin sued the city, a suit she ultimately won. Tanks were built in the Cherry Beach area.

But there was little doubt that the real reason for Joy's difficulty in penetrating the lucrative Toronto market was the "big boys" who made up the so-called oil trust. At the pump motorists could buy the top grade of Joy gasoline, manufactured from Texas oil and transported to Canada from the Gulf of Mexico by ship, nearly 6¢ below the competition's comparable grade retailing for 20.5¢ a gallon. Incidentally, in case you were wondering, 20.5¢ a gallon is equivalent to a little over 4¢ a litre, but with cigarettes 10 for a dime and steak 22¢ a pound, the 1938 vs 1998 comparison, though intriguing, is unfair.

Joy Gasoline newspaper ad from 1938.

Joy Oil was popular for several decades, but soon a variety of names, Hercules, Premium, DX, and OLCO, to name a few, began to show up on the former Joy outlets. The ultimate disposition of the Joy Oil Company is unknown. Anyone know?

Today, except for the station at the corner of Lake Shore Boulevard at Windermere Avenue, all of Joy's unique little buildings are gone.

Thanks to service station buff, Bill Blair for his help with this column.

SANTA CLAUS ALWAYS WELCOME IN TORONTO

November 15, 1998

There are lots of things that make this city great. Things like a great police force, a great fire department, lots of clean drinking water, a safe and efficient transit system, and so on. Then there are those things that are a little more difficult to define, but without them, the city would definitely be a less desirable place to live. Things like the little Island ferryboats, the TTC's red and white streetcars, plenty of parks and trees, and streets without potholes.

Hundreds of "kids" gather on Albert and James streets to cheer Santa as he arrives, led by the band of the famous 48th Highlanders, at Eaton's main store sometime in the 1950s. Note the CBC television cameras to the right. Toronto got its first TV station in 1952. Eaton's Annex is now the site of the Bell building on Bay Street.

One other thing that makes Toronto a special place is the annual Santa Claus Parade, with the 93rd edition taking place this very day.

The very first Santa Claus Parade wasn't really much of parade at all. It consisted of a single vehicle in which Santa was a passenger as it puttered from the old Union Station on Front Street a few steps west of York to the Eaton store, which was located at the northwest corner of Yonge and Queen streets. Along the route the jolly old elf threw handfuls of candy and surprise packages to the curious crowd that gathered to witness the passage of this innovative Eaton's promotion. Obviously it wasn't a coincidence that a happy place called Toyland had just opened in the company store.

The concept of the Santa Claus Parade originated with company founder Timothy Eaton. Following the patriarch's death in 1907, son John Craig Eaton, who recognized the immense promotional possibilities of the event, saw to it that the parade got better and better in succeeding years.

A major promotional coup was achieved in 1923 when Santa's sleigh arrived on city streets pulled by eight live reindeer specially imported from Dr. Wilfrid Grenville's hospital and mission in Labrador for the occasion. The event was covered by newspapers far and wide, and of course the name Eaton's was always mentioned somewhere in the story.

Four years later the parade had expanded to a total of seven floats, and in 1953, a mechanized float depicting Santa in a sleigh pulled by eight prancing reindeer leaping over snow-covered housetops was introduced. This distinctive float is still the parade's trademark.

But as popular as the parade had become, by the early 1980s its future was in doubt. Finally, in a press release issued by the company in early 1982, it was confirmed that the popular event was about to go the way of cheap gasoline and the 25¢ newspaper. Eaton's had found the parade too expensive to continue, and as a result the 1981 Santa Claus Parade would be the last one sponsored by Eaton's. Things certainly looked bleak for the future of this long-time Toronto tradition.

But no sooner had the sad announcement been made than a group of city businessmen, prodded by then Metro Toronto Chairman Paul Godfrey (wonder what he's doing now?), quickly came to the rescue, and on Sunday, November 14, 1982, the "new" Metro Toronto Santa Claus Parade stepped off right on cue.

This year's parade, now the largest of its kind on the continent with its 24 animated floats, 22 bands, and more than 1 300 costumed participants, will have an extra-special surprise for kids of all ages. Warner Brothers Entertainment Inc. is sponsoring a *Wizard of Oz* float complete with Dorothy, Scarecrow, Tin Woodman, Cowardly Lion, and that terrifying hair- (and house-) raising tornado. The entry honours the return to local movie screens of my favourite movie of all time, the *Wizard of Oz*.

The film was first shown here in Toronto at the Loew's (now Elgin) on Yonge Street nearly six decades ago, but for various reasons its popularity was just so-so. However, with the re-release in 1949 (the year I saw the film at the now demolished Alhambra Theatre on Bloor Street west of Bathurst — after several viewings I had to be forcibly retrieved by my father), the movie took off.

The 1998 re-re-release has been digitally restored with the soundtrack remastered in stereo, all modern-day techniques that would have been a mystery to Dorothy, the Munchkins, Glinda, and even the Wicked Witch of the West. In fact, to everyone except the Wizard of Oz himself.

As a kid, I saw the *Wizard of Oz* in my neighbourhood theatre, the Alhambra, which stood for years on the north side of Bloor Street just west of Bathurst. It's now the site of a Swiss Chalet restaurant. This photo was taken in 1941, the year I was born.

TIMELY COTTAGE DOWN BY THE BAY

December 13, 1998

A modern TTC streetcar glides by the "ancient" Ashbridge House, 1998. This vehicle lives in the car house across the street from the house, property that was still covered with water when the old house was new.

Scattered throughout the "new" City of Toronto, which, incidentally, will celebrate its first birthday this coming New Year's Day (and the sky has yet to fall), are a number of beautiful old residences, several of which have been lovingly restored so that visitors may learn about the way people lived and spent their leisure time in years gone by. In the old city are places such as Mackenzie House on Bond Street, Colborne Lodge in High Park, and Spadina House next door to the castle. In North York there's Gibson House, while East York has the historic houses of Todmorden Mills, and York has the partially restored Lambton Tavern. Out in Etobicoke, Montgomery's Inn welcomes visitors, as does the Cornell House in Scarborough.

Add to that list another "ancient" residence, which, through the wisdom and concern for heritage demonstrated by its owners, will soon have a new lease on life. Donated to the people of Ontario by the descendants of the building's original owner, the future of Ashbridge House on Queen Street East is in the hands of the Ontario

Heritage Foundation, which is developing plans for an appropriate and practical reuse of this long-time city landmark.

The Ashbridge name first appears on maps of the area around the little Town of York (which became the City of Toronto in 1834) not long after the family arrived from Pennsylvania. The widow Ashbridge had made up her mind to emigrate with her family to the safety of British North America after ongoing problems, religious and secular, had finally made life intolerable for the fatherless family living in what had become, following the War of Independence (or Revolutionary War, the choice of names dependent on whose side you were on), the newly established United States of America. Sarah's decision to get out was not unusual. Thousands of others, believing they, too, would be better off continuing to live under the rule of King George III than face an uncertain future in the new country, also emigrated northward.

Sarah Ashbridge, accompanied by a substantial entourage consisting of two unmarried sons, one unmarried daughter and two that were married plus their husbands and children, made their way from the Susquehanna River arriving at Niagara (now Niagara-on-the-Lake) in 1793. Hearing that Governor Simcoe was planning to move the capital of his newly established province of Upper Canada from Niagara to a less vulnerable site on the north side of the lake, the family selected a couple of 100-acre lots east of the new townsite. This property had frontage on a sheltered body of water that soon became known as Ashbridge's Bay.

Time passed, and the Ashbridge name became well-known both locally as well as throughout all of York County. It was in 1853 that Sarah's 28-year-old grandson Jesse commissioned architect Joseph Sheard (who was to serve a stint as Toronto's mayor from 1871 to 1872) design a small brick cottage to be erected at the south end of the family farm fronting on what had become known as the Kingston Road (since that's where it led), a thoroughfare that is now part of Queen Street East.

Records indicate that while the cottage was actually built in 1854, it wasn't lived in for another couple of years following Jesse's marriage to Harriet Trainer. She died soon after, and it was Jesse's second wife, Elizabeth, who initiated the idea of landscaping the property, a feature still very much in evidence each growing season.

The appearance of the old farmhouse itself didn't change until 1899, when a second floor was added, followed a couple of decades later by a two-storey addition. It was about this time that the property surrounding the house was subdivided, streets laid out, and many of the present houses built.

Members of the Ashbridge family continued to reside in the old house at 1444 Queen Street East until it, and much of the surrounding property, was donated to the Ontario Heritage Foundation in trust for the citizens of Ontario. As this article is being written a new tenant for this historic property is being sought. Any ideas?

WHEN THE SNOW REALLY WAS WAISTDEEP

December 20, 1998

Pedestrians are almost hidden behind huge piles of snow at the Yonge and King,
December 12, 1944.

Scheduling deadlines here at the Sunday *Sun* make it necessary for me to prepare my columns a week or so before they actually appear. Such lead time could cause problems. For example, I'm writing this story on December 12, a rather interesting date in the city's history. It was on that day in 1944, exactly 54 years ago, that the snow finally stopped falling, having blanketed the unsuspecting city with 520.7 mm (20.5 inches) of the white stuff. It was the worst 24-hour snowstorm in the city's history.

I certainly hope that figure is still in the record books since this story is being written eight days before you'll have an opportunity to read it. Going on the assumption that I didn't put the whammy on things and the long-standing record still stands, let's take a look back at that snowy December 54 years ago.

As usual there was lots of hustle and bustle around town as Torontonians got ready for Christmas. But unlike today, the Christmas of 1944 wouldn't be a cheerful time for everyone. In fact, it was the sixth time in a row that the happiness usually found throughout the nation as the holiday season approached was again overshadowed by a world at war. Later in the month, as families gathered for that special dinner, thousands would be missing, many of whom would never return.

Early in the evening of Monday, December 11, 1944, snow began falling, lightly at first, but soon it was coming down pretty good. Obviously the light flurries predicted in the day's official weather forecast were an understatement.

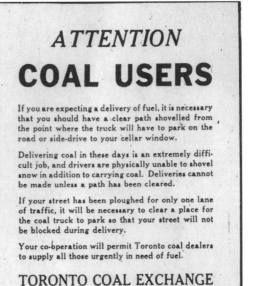

ATTENTION

COAL USERS

If you are expecting a delivery of fuel, it is necessary that you should have a clear path shovelled from the point where the truck will have to park on the road or side-drive to your cellar window.

Delivering coal in these days is an extremely difficult job, and drivers are physically unable to shovel snow in addition to carrying coal. Deliveries cannot be made unless a path has been cleared.

If your street has been ploughed for only one lane of traffic, it will be necessary to clear a place for the coal truck to park so that your street will not be blocked during delivery.

Your co-operation will permit Toronto coal dealers to supply all those urgently in need of fuel.

TORONTO COAL EXCHANGE
ADELAIDE 5961   319 BAY STREET

Most of Toronto's coal companies belonged to the Toronto Coal Exchange. In this ad, which ran shortly after the big storm, the Exchange is imploring customers to make the beleaguered delivery man's job as easy as possible.

Actually, one good thing brought on as a result of the war (as if there's anything good about war) was that gas and tire rationing had become part of everyday life. As a result, automobile and truck traffic throughout the city was much less than in prewar days. To pick up the slack, the TTC had more than 900 streetcars and hundreds of buses ready to serve the needs of the community. (The Yonge subway was still a decade in the future.) As the snow began to pile up, the Commission decided to call out its huge electric sweepers, equipped with massive revolving brushes that threw the snow well away from the tracks, and in doing so managed to bury cars abandoned along each route. As the morning of the twelfth arrived, it began snowing heavier than ever, and soon more streets became impassable. By morning, the city was virtually paralyzed, with just a couple of streetcar lines able to continue operating throughout the storm. Sections of these lines, however, became impassable, as well, with portions of several routes in the outlying districts (Dundas, out near Runnymede Road, and the Weston and Kingston Road routes) out of service during that morning's rush hour. All of the bus routes were affected, with the Hill (serving the Forest Hill district) and Mt. Pleasant lines the first to return to full service later in the day. It was a frantic time for the city's public transportation system.

When the snow finally came to an end, the mammoth task of cleaning up began. In addition to the TTC's mechanical forces, the city's street cleaning department had 1 000 of its men operating more than 150 trucks (50 of which were privately owned) plus 23 snowploughs hard at work desperately trying to reopen main and side streets so that citizens could to get back to work. It was especially important that those who were employed at the various war-related establishments in and around town, GECO at Eglinton and Pharmacy, Inglis on Strachan Avenue, the shipbuilding yards at the foot of Spadina, and the many smaller factories in Leaside, to name just a few, get back to work as soon as possible. Victory couldn't be put off just because of some snow.

As the clean-up got underway, it was revealed that a new 24-hour snowfall record had just been set. Officially set at 20.5 inches, the amount replaced the March 28, 1876, total of a mere 16.2 inches.

Mayor Fred Conboy warned those over 50 against shovelling the heavy snow. At least 13 Torontonians failed to heed his suggestion, suffered heart attacks, and fell dead in the snow. Huge piles of snow blocked side streets, resulting in curtailed home delivery of bread and milk. Families were advised to retrieve their supplies from the local fire hall. Home heating was also affected, with customers of companies such as Elias Rogers, Weaver, and Dominion Coal requested through newspaper and radio ads (TV ads were still years in the future) to clear a path from the curb to the coal chute. Otherwise the beleaguered coal delivery man would simply pass them by. For days after the storm schools remained closed, and supplies in the local grocery stores became more and more scarce.

Eventually things returned to normal, and the scramble to get on with holiday preparations resumed with increased vigour. Stores were soon out of such popular children's gifts as 49¢ miniature soldier sets (8 foot soldiers or 5 mounted), 18-inch-tall dressed dolls at 29¢ each, replica Servicemen's Regulation Helmets for the "let's pretend soldier," 39¢ each, Junior Wireless Sets, $1.95, and the original "Take It or Leave It" board game, $1.98.

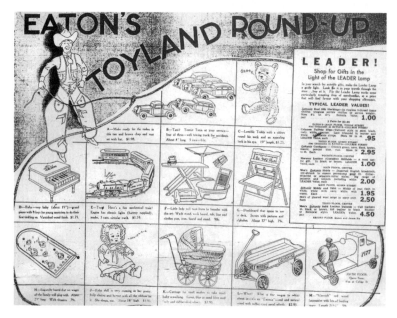

The snow was barely off the main roads when Eaton's ran this ad for its Toyland gift specials.

OUT WITH THE NEW, IN WITH THE OLD

December 27, 1998

No doubt, many of you are getting ready to ring out the old year and welcome the new. Some will spend New Year's evening at friends' homes, while for others it'll be a quiet evening at home. Hundreds will skate in the new year at the ice rink at Harbourfront, and some will opt for a lavish meal at one of the many fancy restaurants or hotel dining rooms around town.

Sunnyside's Club Esquire was one of the city's most popular dance halls. In later years it was known as the Club Top Hat. The building was demolished in the mid-1950s to make way for the Parkside Drive underpass at the Gardiner Expressway.

There was a time, back in the 1940s and 1950s, when the in thing for couples to do each New Year's Eve was to spend the night at one of the many halls and auditoriums around town and dance in each new year to the sounds of the big bands. The list of Toronto's dance halls was a lengthy one. While I'm sure to miss one or two, let me remind you of some of the most popular. There was the good old Palais Royale down at Sunnyside, and the nearby Palace Pier, then located in the Township of Etobicoke. The Palais is still there, of course, and still swings and sways to the sound of the big bands most weekends. The place started life as a boat-building factory operated by Walter Dean. When Sunnyside Amusement Park opened in 1922, Walter was forced to move his operations into the basement when the main floor was turned into a dance hall. Over the years, some of the world's best bands performed there (virtually every big band with the exception of Glenn Miller's), with the all-time record for crowds trying to squeeze into the place being set by Eddy Duchin. In the big-band era, Art Hallman and his Orchestra were often found in attendance.

An interior view of the dance pavilion on the Island at Hanlan's Point, June, 1928.

The Palace Pier, on the other hand, started life, on the drawing boards at least, as an amusement, dance hall, and auditorium complex modeled on the famous Palace Pier in Brighton, England. It was to be a half-mile-long structure poking out a full half mile into Lake Ontario from the west bank of the Humber River. For a variety of reasons, the original idea didn't quite pan out. All that Toronto and the Pier's disappointed shareholders got was a 300-foot-long auditorium that for the longest time didn't know what it wanted to be. Most will remember it in its latter years as a popular dance hall, where Trump Davidson and his band thrilled crowds for many years. In early 1963, an arsonist burned the place down.

Dine or Dance by the Lake

PALAIS ROYALE
SUNNYSIDE BEACH

LUNCHEON .75—TABLE D'HOTE DINNER $1.00

SPECIAL CHICKEN DINNER $1.50

A LA CARTE SERVICE
Beverage License

Dancing Every Evening From
9 o'clock
WITH THE FAMOUS
J. Wilson Jardine and His Palais Royale Orchestra

PLEASURE CANOES—ROWBOATS—PARASOLS

SPECIAL CONVENTION FACILITIES

BANQUETS—DINNER PARTIES

Auto Bus Service
FROM 6:30 P.M. AND HALF HOURLY AFTER. THE GRAY LINE SUNNY-
SIDE SERVICE OPERATE DIRECTLY FROM DOWNTOWN HOTELS
TO OUR MAIN ENTRANCE

FOR RESERVATIONS   PHONE LAKESIDE—0234

Manager

Another popular place for dancing was, and still is, Sunnyside's Palais Royale. This building was a canoe manufacturing factory before being converted into a dance hall in 1922.

Still at Sunnyside there was the Club Esquire on the north side of Lake Shore Boulevard, at the corner of Parkside Drive, a place that was known as the Club Top Hat, until its removal in the mid-1950s for the Gardiner Expressway. And just up the Humber River was the Silver Slipper, which some may have known in later years as the Club Kingsway, with Ozzie Williams on the bandstand.

In other parts of town on New Year's Eve dancers would make a beeline for the Club Embassy at Bloor and Belair, where the house band for years was that of Ferdy Mowry with the perennial Frank Bogart at the piano. Others visited Columbus Hall on the west side of Sherbourne Street, just south of Bloor, where Jack Evans and his orchestra could be found. Jack was also a summertime favourite at Sunnyside's outdoor dance floor, the Seabreeze, not a particularly nice place to be on a cold and snowy New Year's Eve. Many headed for the Orange Hall on College at Euclid, featuring Bob McCaw's band, or Mutual Arena on Mutual Street just south of Dundas, where Bert Niosi ("the Canadian Benny Goodman") and his orchestra often performed. Incidentally, Mutual was the only place in Toronto at which Glenn Miller ever performed.

Up at Yonge and Davenport, there was the Auditorium (officially the Masonic Temple's auditorium) with Paul Firman's band often in attendance.

While large hotels such as the Royal York and King Edward had special attractions on New Year's Eve, many of the city's smaller hotels drew the crowds on New Year's Eve, as well. The Spadina Hotel at King and Spadina had its popular Cabana Room, while further downtown visitors to the Barclay Hotel on Front Street West at Simcoe Street danced the old year away in the Indigo and Flamingo rooms.